Reflecti... ...

Prayers *from*

The
Valley *of the*
Shadow
of Cancer

～ A Personal Prayer Notebook ～
Eleanor M. Bouwman

Published by Creative Bound Inc.
Box 424, Carp, Ontario
Canada K0A 1L0
(613) 831-3641

ISBN 0-921165-50-1
Printed and bound in Canada

Unless otherwise stated, all Bible quotations are taken from The New International Version, © 1984 International Bible Society, published by Zondervan Publishing House.
Back cover quotation by Norman Vincent Peale, *The Power of Positive Thinking*, © 1952 by Prentice-Hall, Inc.

Book design by Wendelina O'Keefe
Front cover photograph by Diarama Stock Photos Inc.

Cataloguing in Publication Data

Bouwman, Eleanor M.
    Reflections : prayers from the valley of the shadow of cancer

ISBN 0-921165-50-1

    1. Cancer—Patients—Prayer-books and devotions.
2. Cancer—Religious aspects—Christianity. I. Title.

BV270.B68 1998   242'.4   C98-900169-5

What Cancer Cannot Do

Cancer is so limited . . .
It cannot cripple love
It cannot shatter hope
It cannot corrode faith
It cannot eat away peace
It cannot destroy confidence
It cannot kill friendship
It cannot shut out memories
It cannot silence courage
It cannot invade the soul
It cannot reduce eternal life
It cannot quench the Spirit
It cannot lessen the power of the resurrection.

Reprinted with permission from *Our Daily Bread*,
copyright 1989 by RBC Ministries, Grand Rapids, MI.

Acknowledgments

I am grateful to God for caring for me and walking by my side as I continue my journey in the Valley. His promises are true in every situation; I can trust Him fully.

I also thank my husband Merv for his ongoing love, prayers and support as I battle cancer.

My gratitude goes to my children, David and Anita, who continue to encourage me and try to keep me laughing.

I am grateful for the professional care and advice I have received from all the doctors and surgeons who have assisted me in my fight against cancer.

Special thanks to Frank Friedrich for his invaluable suggestions in editing this manuscript.

Thanks also to Ruth Taylor, R.N., for sharing her experiences in the chemotherapy section of this book.

I wish to express my gratitude to Pastors Greg Kjos and Garry Remus and to Ray Matthey, chairman of the Saunders-Matthey Foundation for Breast Cancer Research, for reading my manuscript and writing reviews.

As always, I owe much gratitude to all who faithfully intercede for me. May they be richly blessed by our Lord.

Contents

III. Reflections & Prayers When in Need of:

IV. Reflections & Prayers of Thanksgiving for These Blessings:

Introduction

❧❧❧

*F*or many years I would never have considered using prayers written by someone else. To me, praying was a matter of talking to God in my own words; hence, "ready made" prayers seemed unnecessary, even somewhat inferior. However, in recent years, while the vast majority of my prayers are still my own words spoken as a child talking to the Father, I have come to appreciate the prayers of others who share my Christian faith.

The publication of my first book, *The Valley of the Shadow of Cancer*, brought me in contact with many cancer patients. The support group which I began focuses on prayer and sharing. From the experiences of these people and from my own struggles, I have learned not only how vital prayer is, but also how difficult praying can be during the emotional trauma, confusion and pain of living with a deadly disease. In this book I have dealt with many of the hard issues which cancer patients and their families know all too well. I consider it a prayer notebook for people coping with cancer.

I have learned to stay in my "box for today," living every day to the fullest in gratitude to God for the miracle of each new day. Without God's love, promises and His answers to prayer, my walk in the Valley would be one of utter despair and hopelessness.

This is not a book to be read from cover to cover at one sitting; my recommendations for using it are as follows. Choose a topic which is relevant to your immediate situation. After reading my reflection, spend some time contemplating the help you have received from God in similar circumstances. Next, meditate on the scripture passages, asking God to speak to you through them. Perhaps some passages should be memorized. Before you pray the prayer, read it first and delete anything with which you feel uncomfortable or which is irrelevant to your current situation. Each case is unique, so at times there will be aspects of the prayer you need not pray. Then use the blank lines to jot down your own needs about which you wish to pray. Finally, talk to God, using the printed prayer and your notes as guidelines. You will notice the prayers are open-ended (they do not end with "…in Jesus' name. Amen.") so you can easily add your own thoughts. This is *your* prayer notebook for *your* battle with cancer. Please do not feel intimidated by the prayers. They have been fine-tuned to meet the needs of the many people who will use this book. Your own prayers need not be elaborate. My personal prayers in times of trouble are very simple, sometimes merely, "Help!"

I pray that our loving Heavenly Father will hear and answer your prayers and mine, sustaining us as we continue our journey in the Valley of the Shadow of Cancer.

Reflections & Prayers
for God's Help in Dealing with:

Cancer Diagnosis
Chemotherapy
Radiation Treatments
Death Sentence
Doctor Error, Misdiagnosis
Food Cravings
Losses
Nausea
Pain
Sleeplessness
Telling Family and Friends
Upcoming Surgery (general anesthesia)
Upcoming Surgery (local anesthesia)
Weariness
Weight Loss

Cancer Diagnosis

*T*he words "you have cancer" are among the most devastating, terrifying and unbelievable three words that could ever be spoken to you. Those three words have the power to change your life forever. The shock immediately catapults some people into denial; others are completely overwhelmed by waves of grief and despair.

No matter how many people you have known with cancer, it is in a totally different realm when it's a personal diagnosis. However, you must remember that seldom, if ever, does anyone die on the day of receiving the diagnosis; further more, many people become cancer survivors. There is still hope, even though you are entering a very frightening "battle zone."

On first learning of my cancer in the spring of 1989, I experienced fear and disappointment. Many friends had joined Merv and me in praying that the tumor would be benign. It was God's peace that helped me to accept the horrendous news of the malignancy without going into shock or denial. I believed with my whole heart that even with a diagnosis of cancer, God would be with me; indeed, He has been.

Psalm 112:7-8
He will have no fear of bad news; his heart is steadfast, trusting in the Lord. His heart is secure, he will have no fear; in the end he will look in triumph on his foes.

Isaiah 41:10
So do not fear, for I am with you; do not be dismayed, for I am your God. I will strengthen you and help you; I will uphold you with my righteous right hand.

Psalm 31:24
Be strong and take heart, all you who hope in the Lord.

Psalm 50:15
And call upon me in the day of trouble;
I will deliver you, and you will honor me.

Psalm 16:1
Keep me safe, O God, for in you I take refuge.

O Lord, words are inadequate to explain my devastation. I HAVE CANCER. I have joined the ranks of those who are battling this wretched disease. I know many of them personally, but right now I can only think of me—not even my family and friends—just me. I am the one with this terrifying, disgusting, life-changing disease called cancer.

You claim to be the Way, the Truth and the Life, so I cry out to You from this pit.

O Lord, You are the Way and I need You to lead me. The world I have just entered consists of hospitals, clinics, tests, biopsies, surgeries, chemotherapy, radiation treatments, IVs, pain and despair. Only You are able to guide me along the path that lies ahead. I need to lean on Your strong arm. Thank you for showing me the Way.

O God of Truth, let me face my disease honestly. Protect me from denial. If I convince myself nothing is wrong, there is no need to seek healing from You, nor investigate the lifestyle changes You may require of me. Let me grasp the gravity of my situation without fear or denial. Thank you for Your Truth.

Lord, You also said You are the Life, and now I need Your life to give me hope. Thank you for showing me that You are alive, always ready to hear and answer my prayers. Thank you for being the Life.

You say, "Come unto me, all you who labour and are heavy laden, and I will give you rest" (Matthew 11:28). Give me a living faith so I will know beyond a shadow of a doubt that You are speaking those words to me. Cancer is such a heavy burden and I need You to carry it for me, so I may enter into Your rest.

O God of miracles, I pray for healing, peace and joy. I believe You will provide them as you see fit. Produce in me patience to wait for

Your timing instead of pushing for my agenda, which is to be healed immediately and get on with life. Usually that's not how You work, so teach me Your wisdom as I walk with You.

Lord, sometimes fear seems to engulf me. In those moments let me, like the sinking Peter, keep my eyes fixed on You.

Despair also seems to be just one breath away. When I feel overwhelmed by it, hold me in Your arms and keep me safe.

Thank you for not abandoning me. Help me lest I perish in fear, anguish and utter hopelessness. Cancer has completely changed my plans, hopes, dreams—my whole life!

O Lord, I thank You for the peace and courage I already feel as I look to You and hear Your words, "My grace is sufficient for you, for my power is made perfect in weakness" (2 Corinthians 12:9). I need You, Lord, more than ever before!

Chemotherapy

I am often asked my reasons for never having had chemotherapy. When I first contracted kidney cancer, my doctors said there was no chemo for that kind of cancer, so obviously it wasn't offered. When the lymph nodes removed at the time of my breast surgery were free of cancer, again chemo was not an option. However, when kidney cancer metastasized, my oncologist did recommend chemotherapy. I refused, having been advised earlier of its ineffectiveness for kidney cancer, a fact also confirmed by my own reading and research. When I informed my oncologist that I knew it was ineffective for my cancer, she agreed. (Merv and I were shocked to be offered a therapy as toxic as chemo by a doctor who knew it wouldn't work!) I stuck with my decision, refusing chemotherapy to fight kidney cancer.

What follows are the reflections of two friends who have taken chemotherapy.

One woman, who has since died, told me that when her oncologist recommended more chemo just after her hair was beginning to grow again, she told him in utter desperation that she would scratch out his eyes if she lost her hair again! Needless to say, loss of hair was very traumatic for her.

Another friend shared:

"Having been a nurse who had administered chemo, I found being on the receiving end an unbelievable experience. My nursing instinct was to follow the chemo route to fight my non Hodgkin's lymphoma, completely unaware of alternative therapies. However, within a day of diagnosis, for whatever reason, I also realized I needed to change my diet to one of more fruits and vegetables. This drew criticism from family and friends who felt it was lacking adequate protein.

"Shortly thereafter, a colleague of my husband gave him a brown grocery bag containing many books about alternative medicine. They were from his wife, Eleanor, the author of this book. The information in that brown bag changed the direction of my cancer management. In spite of being very skeptical initially, I followed those suggestions which made sense to me, including buying organic foods to give my body superior nutrition. My husband supported me in my battle to regain my health.

"Being well aware of the side effects of chemo, my great fear was loss of hair. Of course, I hoped to be the exception; three weeks later I was bald! It was both devastating and overwhelming to have my children and husband see me. Thank goodness for a stylish wig that suited me well. On hot days it felt like a winter cap, so a light turban became a great substitute. In the "year of the wig" I began appreciating the hours of routine hair care I had saved.

"Having heard of chemo patients whose hair had grown back curlier or thicker in texture, my hopes were high. Unfortunately, instead of my natural brown color, my hair grew back a stark white! I was not prepared to be a white-haired, middle-aged woman, so my search for a natural hair coloring product began. I became a birch blonde, thanks to an herbal preparation which contained no chemicals.

"Several years have passed and even though I feel well and remain cancer-free, I continue to put into practice the lifestyle and diet changes I made when battling cancer. Looking back, I am thankful I had chemotherapy to help fight my specific cancer."

Psalm 32:7
*You are my hiding place; you will protect me from
trouble and surround me with songs of deliverance.*

Psalm 62:5-8
*Find rest, O my soul, in God alone; my hope comes from him.
He alone is my rock and my salvation; he is my fortress,
I will not be shaken. My salvation and my honor
depend on God; he is my mighty rock, my refuge.
Trust in him at all times, O people; pour out your
hearts to him, for God is our refuge.*

O Lord my Saviour, help me in my distress. I am too sick to pray, so I depend on Your mercy and the intercessions of my friends to provide courage to persevere this day. Protect me from the awful side effects of this treatment. Grant me Your healing and let me feel Your love as I rest in You.

(Feel free to enlist the prayer support of your family and friends when you are too ill to pray.)

Radiation Treatments

W
hen battling breast cancer, the thought of having radiation beamed at my body was very frightening, as well as confusing. Ordinarily I would be cautioned to avoid the very nuclear energy that would bombard my sick body. Does that make any sense? In answer to my many questions, I was assured that even though healthy cells would be damaged, they would recover after a time. The abnormal cancer cells would be permanently damaged; they would die. Since my aim was to rid my body of all cancer, that explanation seemed reasonable and after much prayer, I consented to the therapy.

The huge machine intimidated me, but the information I had acquired put me at ease. Many patients do not feel free to ask questions, so they have very little knowledge of what will happen to them. This has never been my way of dealing with the complexities of fighting cancer.

Since my safety depended largely on the proper functioning of the radiotherapy machine and the expertise of the technicians, I always prayed during the treatments. I also asked God to be my shield of protection.

Psalm 7:10
My shield is God Most High, who saves the upright in heart.

Psalm 28:7a
*The Lord is my strength and my shield; my heart
trusts in him, and I am helped.*

Psalm 33:20
We wait in hope for the Lord; he is our help and our shield.

O Lord, another radiation treatment is scheduled for today, making my body the target of nuclear energy again. Be with me in a mighty way and shield me from all harm. Prevent the machine from delivering an overdose of deadly radiation and protect my healthy cells from irreparable damage. Lord, You know where the cancer cells are, so please let them be annihilated by the radiation. Minimize the side effects and let me be grateful for this technology.

Forgive my impatience when these weeks of therapy seem to be going so slowly. Teach me how to arrange my schedule to accommodate these daily interruptions. May my hope and trust in You prevent discouragement and discontentment from taking root.

Now I place my life and health in Your care once again, knowing You are able to do more than I could ever imagine.

I love You, Lord. You are my Provider and Protector.

Death Sentence

When my oncologist gave me a "six-month death sentence," Merv and I were devastated. I felt like a convict on Death Row, for where else are people told how much longer they have to live? After the initial shock we became angry. How could another human being put a time limit on my life and rob me of my hope of healing? I had not asked for any indication of how long I might live, and yet I was told. Thank God for friends who prayed for us immediately and my holistic physician for his advice to reject it as a curse.

That happened in March 1995. Even though my battle with kidney cancer continues, it has not given me one sick day, nor have I taken any cancer medication since that time. Doctors do make mistakes and God is able to intervene miraculously!

Alternative protocols such as adhering to a strict diet, taking vitamins, supplements, enzymes, antioxidants, etc., and walking and rebounding regularly are my ways of fighting my disease. To help me in this, many people pray for me as I seek God's guidance, wisdom and healing.

Even though CAT scans, taken in June 1996 and June 1997, showed several metastatic tumors in my liver and renal bed and lymphatic involvement around my pancreas, I still feel completely healthy. Medically speaking, there is no hope of recovery, yet God gives His peace as I continue my battle. Truly each day is a wonderful gift and I try to live life to the fullest, giving Him the glory.

If a doctor has predicted the time of your death, remember only God knows the number of days He has allotted to you. Make the most of every day He gives you. Do not let a mere mortal rob you of hope! If, however, you realize through your suffering that your time here on earth is indeed short, rejoice in God's promise of eternal life to all who believe in Jesus Christ as their Lord and Savior.

Psalm 139:16b
*All the days ordained for me were written in
your book before one of them came to be.*

Psalm 18:4-6
*The cords of death entangled me; the torrents of destruction
overwhelmed me. The cords of the grave coiled around me;
the snares of death confronted me. In my distress I called to
the Lord; I cried to my God for help. From his temple
he heard my voice; my cry came before him, into his ears.*

Romans 14:8
*If we live, we live to the Lord; and if we die, we die to the Lord. So,
whether we live or die, we belong to the Lord.*

Psalm 23:4
*Even though I walk through the valley of the shadow of death,
I will fear no evil, for you are with me;
your rod and your staff, they comfort me.*

O Father, they say I'm dying! Sorrow overwhelms me as "six months" becomes my life. I had thought I wasn't afraid to die, but this is so hard to accept and I am afraid. Lord, I give You this crushing burden of fear.

My doctor is playing God and that makes me angry. She has no right to rob me of the hope and peace You have given. Even if the prognosis is accurate, I am outraged at the arrogance of someone predicting the time of my death. My life and death are in Your hands, not my doctor's. Forgive my anger and forgive my doctor for telling me what I did not ask.

Lord, if death really is drawing near, I know You will comfort and prepare me to take that step from time into eternity. You will also sustain my family with Your loving care. However, You know I want to spend more time with them. Please let that "six months" be a mistake. Please heal me. Please save me and make me whole. I feel as though I am sinking beneath an unbearable load of sorrow and despair, yet I know You will stay with me and carry my load. Grant me grace and faith to live or to die according to Your will. I say with St. Paul, "For me to live is Christ, to die is gain" (Philippians 1:21).

Doctor Error, Misdiagnosis

❧❧

*F*orgiving is easy when the stakes are low. But what about forgiving a doctor whose misdiagnosis or error has caused you much pain and anguish, or worse, minimized your chances for survival? Suddenly, forgiving becomes something you do not want to do, and seems impossible even if you want to. When this happened to me, I wondered if God would really expect me to forgive. A brief remembrance of Jesus on the cross deflated all my arguments against forgiving. He said, "Father, forgive them, for they do not know what they are doing" (Luke 23:34), while he was being slain. He is our example; should we do less?

Forgiveness always reminds me of an incident when our daughter Anita, a very quiet, sensitive child, was in the first grade. One day she came home from school absolutely livid. Her eyes and voice were full of rage as she told me about the boy who had embarrassed her in front of the whole class. I had never seen such hatred in her, so when she finished her tirade and had settled down a bit, I gently reminded her of the need to forgive him. The rage flew back into her eyes as she said, "I will never forgive him!" After remaining quiet for a while, I comforted her, and then suggested that if she refused to forgive, every time she prayed the Lord's Prayer, she was actually telling God not to forgive her sins. Without hesitation she responded, "Then I'll never pray the Lord's Prayer again!" My little daughter was facing a spiritual crisis. After comforting her again, I asked her to go somewhere by herself and talk to Jesus about the whole matter. A short time later she skipped into the kitchen, calm and happy. She grinned and sheepishly said, "I think Jesus wants me to forgive him, so I did." Oh, to be as uncomplicated and obedient as a child!

Colossians 3:13
*Bear with each other and forgive whatever grievances you may
have against one another. Forgive as the Lord forgave you.*

Matthew 6:12
Forgive us our debts, as we also have forgiven our debtors.

Ephesians 4:32
*Be kind and compassionate to one another, forgiving
each other, just as in Christ God forgave you.*

Mark 11:25
*And when you stand praying, if you hold anything
against anyone, forgive him, so that your Father in heaven
may forgive you your sins.*

O God, You commanded us to forgive everyone who wrongs us. My heart knows it would include the doctor whose error has hurt me, but my emotions cry out, "No, I can't." But if I'm honest, I suppose I'm really saying, "No, I won't." So Lord, I come now to receive from You both the desire and ability to forgive my doctor. My sins hurt You infinitely more than he has hurt me, yet You always are willing to forgive me. Please heal the sense of betrayal and anger which has taken root in my soul. Wash my sin, and I will be whiter than snow (Psalm 51:7). Then let me rejoice in my salvation and forgiveness. Remind me that it cost You dearly—death on a cruel cross.

So now, as best I can, I forgive my doctor and I ask You to forgive him, too. Lord, help me guard my heart so no evil thoughts of bitterness or unforgiveness can reenter. Thank you, Lord.

Now please guide me as I plan my next step. Help me understand that choosing a different doctor does not mean I haven't forgiven. Give me Your wisdom to make my choice with a clean heart. Enable me to live in this forgiveness, Father.

Food Cravings

A radical change in diet is probably the most drastic, difficult change required of cancer warriors who have chosen alternative therapies to fight their disease. Such protocols usually have some kind of restrictive diet, usually vegetarian or vegan (no animal products whatsoever). At times it seems all thoughts revolve around food, especially that which is not allowed.

Since embarking on my holistic battle with cancer, my diet has been lacto-ovo-vegetarian (some dairy and eggs) or vegetarian with the addition of occasional small portions of organically raised meat and fish or a gluten-free vegan diet for periods of what I call "heavy-duty detox."

At all times I try to avoid white flour, white rice, coffee and tea (except herbal), all processed foods and those containing chemicals. My fruits and vegetables are organic (grown without chemical fertilizers, pesticides or fungicides), depending on availability and cost. Regular snack foods such as chips, fries, crackers, cookies, most desserts, etc., definitely are not in my diet.

Many books would have us believe that after staying on a particular diet for a few months the cravings and taste for other foods will disappear, but it has not been quite that simple for me. In fact, after several years on a restrictive diet, I still have cravings for forbidden foods; this, even though my pre-cancer eating habits were very healthy. For people whose diets include many empty-calorie junk foods and high-fat animal products, the required dietary changes are extremely hard to accept.

Except during a rigorous detox program, I do allow myself the occasional "treat." My little axiom to which I adhere is: "If I'm going to cheat, it has to be worth it!" Hence, I stray from my diet to eat only that which I really crave. These occasions are very rare, so I refuse to let guilt rob me of the enjoyment the forbidden food provides. I do not believe that a few small coffees or one or two small orders of fries over a whole year will hasten my death. (Besides, I have convinced myself that the extra pleasure will probably increase the flow of endorphins which in turn just might cancel the negative effects of the food in question!)

For me it is actually easier to say "no" to forbidden foods altogether than to make a decision every time I encounter them. That's probably why I've been able to stick to my limited diet so consistently over the years. For family gatherings or potluck meals, I usually take a main course and dessert which fits my diet. This helps me resist the temptation of all that wonderful food.

The purchase of many vegetarian, health-promoting cookbooks is a great encouragement to continue eating in this manner. I don't feel nearly as deprived when preparing new and interesting recipes which will strengthen my immune system. Occasionally, when the restrictions really annoy me, I reread some of the books which outline the benefits of such a diet. That inspires me to continue. Thanking God for the food I may eat goes a long way towards getting rid of my complaints and cravings.

It is of the utmost importance that I give attention to the needs of my spirit as well as my body. My quiet times of Bible study and prayer with the Lord every morning and regular worship in my church feed my spirit and keep me focused on Him and His provisions. Both my body and spirit need the continual nourishment provided by my Heavenly Father.

Matthew 6:25
Therefore I tell you, do not worry about your life,
what you will eat or drink; or about your body, what
you will wear. Is not life more important than food,
and the body more important than clothes?

Proverbs 21:20
In the house of the wise are stores of choice food and oil,
but a foolish man devours all he has.

Isaiah 55:2b
Listen, listen to me, and eat what is good,
and your soul will delight in the richest of fare.

Revelation 3:20
Here I am! I stand at the door and knock.
If anyone hears my voice and opens the door,
I will come in and eat with him, and he with me.

O my Father, I confess my dissatisfaction with the diet my doctor has suggested. There is no food in my cupboards or fridge which interests me today and that is very annoying. I crave cheese (meat, coffee, chips, etc.) and feel deprived because I can't have them. My grumbling has made me ungrateful for your provisions. Forgive this sin and help me remember that even on my restrictive diet, I have much more food than most people in the world. I earnestly repent of my attitude of discontentment and ungratefulness.

So Lord, I choose to thank You right now for the food that is available each day. By Your grace we are able to buy organic foods, even though they are more expensive than regular foods.

Make me willing to accept my diet limitations and help me overcome the cravings I am experiencing. Show me what to eat today.

Remind me also, Lord, that spiritual food is far more important than the physical, for if I neglect that, my spirit will surely wither and die. Let me take time to "devour" Your Word and learn from it. Nourish my spirit when I partake of Your supper—Holy Communion. You are the Bread of Life; I thank and praise You for Your sacrifice. When You knock at the door of my heart I will invite You in to eat with me. Such time spent with You will make these cravings lose their power, and I will be grateful once again for my "daily bread."

Losses

Among the many ramifications of a cancer diagnosis, losses seem overwhelming at times. For some, their loss eventually is loss of life. Others, even though they recover, experience some short-lived or ongoing losses. For me, throughout years of continuing crises, losses have been a very real part of my life in the Valley, but I refuse to dwell on them

My losses include my salary, since on the advice of my holistic physician, I quit my job to wage a full-time cancer battle. That decision not only stopped my paychecks, but also ended payments into my pension fund. However, I choose not to worry about it. Instead, I seek to turn my losses into something for which to be thankful. Though my paychecks have ceased, Merv is able to continue in his job and our needs are met. That causes me to be thankful instead of counting my loss.

Loss of broader social contacts has also been my experience since no longer being a part of the workforce. This partial isolation can lead to a loss of self-esteem. When so many women my age have highly successful careers, my life at home seems rather trite and of much less value.

A good job doesn't make those women more worthwhile, but I still feel awkward and somewhat embarrassed when asked about my job. I then remember the scriptures that assure me of my worth in God's eyes. Furthermore, my reduced social contacts allow more time to spend in prayer for myself and intercessory prayers for others. It also permits me to continue my time-consuming routines like rebounding, juicing and retention enemas. I thank God for making this time available to me. As always, gratitude for what I have gets my mind off what's been lost.

Another loss is the freedom of going to a restaurant to just "grab a bite" (all fast foods are forbidden) or choosing anything I would like from among all those scrumptious dishes at a potluck dinner. This is something I have to deal with frequently and I consider it a great loss. My friends are very considerate when they invite us for a meal and usually try to serve foods I am allowed to eat. I am very grateful for their efforts and many times they surprise themselves when they discover their "gourmet vegetarian chef" abilities. Dining at their tables is always a delightfully nourishing experience.

My physical losses include a kidney, adrenal gland and my spleen. I am thankful that I can live well without them. My physical losses are very minor compared with the loss of a breast or limb which many cancer patients experience.

The progression of my disease has been very unusual in that I have almost always been spared the loss of general well-being. For example, while my disease has been "fourth stage, terminal" for many years now, I usually feel totally well in spite of the metastatic tumors which continue to develop in various parts of my body. Thus, cancer has not robbed me of feeling healthy, and my gratitude to God for His mercy in this vital area is never ending.

Some gains have actually come my way as a direct result of cancer. Through my support group "CANSURVIVE, Days of Encouragement" and my book *The Valley of the Shadow of Cancer*, I have met many wonderful fellow cancer warriors. Our times of sharing and encouraging one another, our prayers for one another and our telephone chats make all the losses in the Valley worthwhile!

If you are suffering losses, God is more than able to turn them into blessings if you allow Him to work in your life. His ways are not our ways, but they are always the best ways.

I take great comfort and joy in knowing that if I eventually lose my life to cancer, it will usher me into eternal life which God promises to those who believe in His Son Jesus as their Savior. That would be the ultimate gain! "For to me, to live is Christ and to die is gain" (Philippians 1:21).

Philippians 3:8a
What is more, I consider everything a loss compared to the surpassing greatness of knowing Christ Jesus my Lord...

Matthew 10:39
Whoever finds his life will lose it, and whoever loses his life for my sake will find it.

Psalm 147:3
He heals the brokenhearted and binds up their wounds.

O most Holy God, I feel so sad today. There have been many changes in my life since I contracted cancer, and it seems I have lost so much. My disease has robbed me of many freedoms: freedom to hold a job, freedom to eat what I desire, freedom to participate in strenuous activities and sometimes even the freedom to be happy and carefree. Lord, forgive me when I choose to dwell on these aspects of my life rather than on Your blessings. Forgive my murmuring and complaining.

Thank you that You have hidden blessings and provisions for me in all my losses. Help me always remember that with You as my Savior, I have everything I could ever need. You are my All in All.

Lord, I now choose to be grateful that You supply my needs even though my job has ceased. Thank you, too, for the faithfulness of my family and friends who stick by me no matter how my disease is affecting me. Bless them with Your love. I am also grateful for Your presence in my loneliness. Give me wisdom and the desire to renounce all thoughts of discouragement, dissatisfaction and self-pity. Draw me ever closer to You, for when I look to You my losses become very insignificant.

(You may wish to make a list of your losses and find something in each for which to be grateful.)

Nausea

People are not created equal where nausea is concerned. Some remain very dignified and quiet (how do they do that?), but I have not been blessed with that ability. My violent gagging is very noisy and forceful, leaving me with bloodshot eyes. Needless to say, I try to avoid it at all costs. (As a child, I once was very nauseated and vomited loudly. My dad, hearing me as he worked in the barnyard, ran to the house to see if an animal was caught somewhere!)

Since I have not had chemotherapy, my periods of nausea have been limited. During the six days between the embolization (killing) of my cancerous kidney and the subsequent surgery, I was very ill. I felt suspended somewhere between life and death. The pain medication upset my stomach. Even though Gravol partially controlled my nausea, it was a very difficult time. When the post-surgery IV was replaced with oral antibiotics, they wreaked havoc with my traumatized stomach, causing the nausea to return. Violent retching with a 23-centimeter (9-inch) incision is one experience I won't forget. I never had to call for a nurse—they always heard me and came running immediately!

Nausea continued after my discharge from the hospital. It was after eating only Astro yogurt (live culture) and buttermilk for twenty-four hours that my stressed digestive system was able to handle food again. However, it took quite some time for my digestion to fully return to normal. For several weeks, whenever I left the house, I took a small bottle of buttermilk with me to curb this recurring problem.

Nausea is not only physically taxing, causing exhaustion and dehydration, but also emotionally devastating. During such times, cancer patients need an abundant supply of encouragement, love and prayers from their family and friends.

Psalm 4:1
Answer me when I call to you, O my righteous God.
Give me relief from my distress; be merciful
to me and hear my prayer.

Psalm 6:2-3
Be merciful to me, Lord, for I am faint; O Lord, heal me,
for my bones are in agony. My soul is in anguish.
How long, O Lord, how long?

Psalm 5:1-2
Give ear to my words, O Lord, consider my sighing.
Listen to my cry for help, my King and my God,
for to you I pray.

*H*oly Father, I am too weak and sick to pray. I beg You to take away my nausea. Heal me quickly.

Show my doctors what will stop my vomiting. Because I need nourishment to fight my disease, this is very discouraging for my family and for me. Help me choose proper foods to aid the healing of my digestive system. Feed my spirit as I await being fed physically.

Lord, I put myself into Your care. Carry me through this horrendously agonizing and painful time. Thank you for all those people who are loving and encouraging me and interceding on my behalf. I know You hear our prayers and I believe You will answer our pleas for help.

(Since praying is next to impossible in these trying situations, invite and allow others to intercede for you.)

Pain

Pain and cancer usually go hand in hand, causing many people incredible suffering due to the invasive and destructive nature of the disease. However, this is one area in which I have been very blessed. With the exception of severe pain when kidney cancer first appeared and limited pain following surgeries, my walk in the Valley has been free from physical pain. This is highly unusual for terminal cancer patients, especially if they have battled their disease as long as I have. Each pain-free day is a wonderful gift from my Lord, and I thank Him for His mercy.

I have known many cancer patients whose extreme pain has reduced their lives to just barely surviving until their next pain medication. Fortunately, when a "pump" is used, the pain control is more constant, allowing them to enjoy times of effective pain reduction.

For some, the pain is chronic and this, too, while perhaps not extreme, can be very debilitating and discouraging. Since pain accompanies many diseases, it is a major problem faced by countless people each day. I ask God for His healing touch as well as for effective pain medications to relieve this suffering.

When pain is intense the mind is totally focused on it, making it very difficult to pray. Therefore, it is of prime importance that others pray continually for their suffering loved ones. God promises to care for the weak and wounded, and I believe He will hear their prayers of intercession. God also promises eternal life with Him where there will be no pain or suffering. That is the blessed hope of everyone who believes that Jesus' suffering, death and resurrection has bought them their pardon and salvation.

Jeremiah 4:19a
Oh, my anguish, my anguish! I writhe in pain.
Oh, the agony of my heart! My heart pounds
within me, I cannot keep silent.

Psalm 69:29
I am in pain and distress; may your salvation,
O God, protect me.

Revelation 21:3-4
And I heard a loud voice from the throne saying, "Now the dwelling of
God is with men, and he will live with them.
They will be his people, and God himself will be with
them and be their God. He will wipe every tear
from their eyes. There will be no more death or mourning or
crying or pain, for the old order of things has passed away."

My God, my God, why have You forsaken me? (Mark 15:34b) Lord, I hurt so badly and this pain has made me so weak I can hardly cope. I need to rely totally on You, for I have no strength of my own. I beg You to remove my pain and heal my aching body. Give my doctors wisdom as they seek to help me.

Forgive me when I doubt Your ability to hear me and care for me. I do know You will answer my prayers in the best way, but this overwhelming pain is an extreme test of my faith. Help me believe that You will never send me more than I can bear.

Lord, please remind others to pray for me now, because I'm just too weary to think. Help me, Lord Jesus. I rest in You.

Sleeplessness

Although the inability to sleep has occasionally been my experience, it has never been an ongoing problem. However, I have learned from many other cancer patients that it is a major source of stress when dealing with this disease. Lying awake as the hours drag by is probably one of the deepest pits of loneliness in the Valley. For whatever reason, the situation always seems most hopeless and terrifying between 1:00 a.m. and 4:00 a.m. When I awaken feeling frightened or discouraged, I listen to a audiotape called *Springs of Comfort* produced by the Sisters of Mary. (I keep a small tape-player with head phones in my bedside table for this purpose.) The Holy Spirit always uses the comforting words and music to lift my spirit and renew my hope.

If I am not fearful or distressed, I fill those wakeful hours with prayer for cancer patients. That focuses my mind on God and the needs of others. My annoyance is not nearly as great when my time of sleeplessness is put to good use.

Psalm 4:8
I will lie down and sleep in peace, for you alone,
O Lord, make me dwell in safety.

Psalm 23:2-3a
He makes me lie down in green pastures,
he leads me beside quiet waters, he restores my soul.

Psalm 63:6-8
On my bed I remember you; I think of you through the watches
of the night. Because you are my help, I sing in the shadow of
your wings. My soul clings to you; your right hand upholds me.

*O*gracious Heavenly Father, You promise sleep to those whom You love (Psalm 127:2b), yet I am again staring into the foreboding darkness. I feel lonely and isolated when everyone else is asleep, but I know You are with me. Thank you for that assurance.

Please protect my mind from frustration or the evil of worry and anxiety concerning my disease.

Forgive my annoyance when time seems to stand still as I repeatedly check the clock. Will morning never come? In Your Holy Word You say, "…weeping may remain for a night, but rejoicing comes in the morning" (Psalm 30:5b). Thank you that no matter how long the night may be, morning will come bringing new mercies (Lamentations 3:22-23). (Spend some time thanking God for your many blessings, for example, home, family, doctors, clothing, salvation, etc.)

Now bring to my mind those who need prayer and let me bless them with my intercessions for them. Hear me and then bring rest and sleep to my weary body. Thank you again for being here in the Valley in the midst of my sleepless loneliness.

Telling Family and Friends

When and how to keep family and friends informed is a difficult issue to be dealt with by every cancer patient. In fact, they first have to decide how much they themselves want to know about their disease and prognosis. I have known some who neither ask questions nor read anything about their condition. I suppose they believe that what they don't know, won't hurt them, and indeed, not knowing may spare them from some premature concerns.

This has never been my way of dealing with cancer. I want to learn as much as possible about my "enemy," always seeking to understand the severity of my situation. However, I never ask my doctors to predict how much longer I will live. Sometimes I begin a consultation by saying, "I want to know how bad it is, but I do not want you to put a time limit on my life." The day I was given a "six-month death sentence" I had neglected to say that because I was not expecting bad news. Only God knows the time of my death, and I find it extremely arrogant for doctors to volunteer that kind of information especially, as in my case, without being asked.

Once I have learned all that I feel is important, I decide when and how much to tell my family. Usually Merv goes with me to crucial medical appointments, so he knows as much as I do. But there have been a few times when he was unable to be there when I received bad news. Then I needed some time alone before I was ready to tell him the whole truth. He didn't like that, but I just had to pray and internalize it before being able to talk about it. After sharing the situation with Merv, I always phoned my brother and sister to keep them informed.

We have always waited for a conclusive diagnosis before telling our children. Both David and Anita were preparing for final college and university exams when I was told I had six months to live. We limited our sharing to a few very close friends, so our children would not hear the news before their exams. Now that both are in their twenties we give them more detailed information than we did when they were young teenagers. As adults living on their own, they are better able to accept all the facts. I am convinced even young children need to know when a loved one has cancer. They can sense the stress in the family, so hiding it only serves to confuse them. They may feel much rejection and anxiety because of the secrecy. However, young children need not be told the grim details.

As for keeping friends informed, those closest to us are given specific information so they can pray for us. Also, they are better able to give our family support if they are aware of our situation. We are truly blessed by these friends who always keep my confidential concerns to themselves and help us in our times of need.

I am very open in informing others of my cancer battle, but details often confuse them. (For example, the mention of tumors in my liver immediately leads them to conclude I have liver cancer. They do not understand that those tumors represent kidney cancer which has metastasized.)

I deal with each situation as it arises, always praying for wisdom before sharing my bad news. If a report has been good, I feel like telling the whole world! Then all who have been praying for me can rejoice with our family and thank God for His mercy and healing.

Proverbs 25:11
A word aptly spoken is like apples of gold in settings of silver.

Proverbs 11:13
A gossip betrays a confidence, but a trustworthy man keeps a secret.

*O*Father of all knowledge, help me cope with this new information concerning my prognosis. At times these facts are too devastating for me to even think about, let alone tell others. However, I know I must share this heavy burden with my loved ones. Please give me the right words when I share this bad news with my husband (children, friends, etc.). Show me how much to tell each one to keep them informed. As my prayer warriors, they need to know my current situation. Lord, I need much wisdom, strength and courage right now.

My God, I beseech You to prepare each of them to receive this news. Comfort us as we adjust our thinking to include this information. Let us keep foremost in our minds that You are the one who has full control of my life, so we really need not fear this report. Remind us of other discouraging times when You lifted us out of the darkness of despair into the light of hope.

(It may help to write the names of those you need to inform, and prayerfully consider what and how you will share with them. Also be sure to tell them which facts are confidential.)

Upcoming Surgery
(general anesthesia)

*F*or me, the most frightening aspect of surgery is that period of 'nothingness' while under anesthesia. I feel very vulnerable, utterly at the mercy of the surgical team, and I wonder if I will awaken from that very unnatural sleep. When anxiety surfaces, striving to stay in my "box for today" is very helpful and I pray much for God's presence and protection.

For some of my surgeries it was confirmed beforehand that the tumor was malignant, while for others the surgery would reveal the nature of the problem. That added more stress, causing me to fear regaining consciousness. I did not want any more bad news.

Psalm 86:6-7
Hear my prayer, O Lord; listen to my cry for mercy. In the day of my trouble I will call to you, for you will answer me.

Luke 23:46b
Father, into your hands I commit my spirit.

Psalm 130:5
I wait for the Lord, my soul waits, and in his word I put my hope.

*F*ather God, my date of surgery looms in front of me, hemming me in on all sides with fears and uncertainties. However, I do have Your peace as I await that day. I pray for Your presence in the operating room, giving Your wisdom as it is needed. Let me feel Your awesome, comforting love as I drift into that very unnatural sleep. Let me rest in You while I am 'sleeping' and protect my mind from evil. Lord, guide the surgeon's hands, making them steady and skilled. Let the support staff be competent as they assist my doctor and attend to my needs. Please cleanse the blood if a transfusion is needed. Let it be free of any contamination.

Protect me from anxiety as I drift in and out of consciousness at the end of my surgery. Give me Your peace no matter what the post-operative diagnosis will be. I thank You that You already know the outcome and are preparing the way for me. Without that assurance I would be frantic. Help me stay in my "box for today" as I await the day of surgery.

Thank you for my country where this medical care is readily available. So, even though I fear my surgery, I choose to be grateful for it.

I ask Your blessings on my family as they pray and comfort each other while I am in the operating room. Give them Your gentle love and calm assurance, so they can rest in You and trust You, no matter what. I say now with Jesus, " Father, into Your hands I commit my spirit" (Luke 23:46).

Upcoming Surgery
(local anesthesia)
❧❧❧

*I*n my many years in the Valley, I have undergone numerous surgeries. For less invasive procedures I much prefer having local anesthesia. It is less stressful than general anesthesia, and I have had several malignant tumors removed in this manner. However, being awake does have a down side; I am aware of exactly what is happening. Even though I feel no pain, my vivid imagination has no trouble envisioning what the surgeon is doing!

Recently a kidney cancer metastatic tumor was removed from my rib cage (the third one at that site). When my surgeon used the cauterizing instrument, I could smell burning flesh—mine! In spite of that, I had peace as I lay there. God has blessed me with a highly skilled, compassionate surgeon, and I am very grateful for his competence.

My prayers before this type of surgery always include asking for wisdom for my doctor, as well as peace of mind for myself. Sometimes my tumors are difficult to remove, and I need extra grace to lie still. Usually I pray silently. This focuses my mind on God, my Healer and Sustainer. I thank Him for being with me even when I'm "under the surgeon's knife."

Psalm 86:7
In the day of my trouble I will call to you, for you will answer me.

Isaiah 26:3
*You will keep in perfect peace him whose mind is
steadfast, because he trusts in you.*

Psalm 94:22
*But the Lord has become my fortress,
and my God the rock in whom I take refuge.*

*M*y Heavenly Father, be my Great Physician as I prepare for surgery. I am thankful it will be minor, without the trauma of being put to sleep. However, I will need a fresh supply of Your grace and Your peace that passes all understanding as I lie there during the procedure. Help me to keep my mind focused on You at all times.

Please bless my doctor with Your wisdom and skill so the operation will successfully rid my body of the cancerous tumor. Once again I thank You for the competence and care of my surgeon.

Lord, I also pray for minimal loss of blood. I am grateful for the speed at which my body has always healed, and I pray now for a rapid recovery once again. Thank you for a country like Canada where this type of medical care is readily available to everyone.

Thank you now for Your mercy, grace and healing. Grant me peace of mind as I await my surgery.

Weariness

Coping with the pain, uncertainty and emotional distress of cancer often produces a profound weariness for both the patient and family. When the exhaustion resulting from surgery, radiation or chemotherapy treatments and countless trips to the cancer clinic are added, it becomes obvious that burnout and discouragement are very common experiences.

There are times when my mind, spirit and body are overwhelmed with weariness and my strength to keep fighting my cancer is all but gone. Then I just quietly sit or lie down while beseeching the Lord to revive me and my family. I have to rely totally on Him to breathe new life and energy into all of us, so we can continue on the path that lies ahead. Without God's help our weariness would strangle us, robbing us of all those positive emotions which are so necessary in our daily coping with cancer.

(At these times friends need to support the family—not just the patient—with whatever help is needed, for example, meals, a break for the caregiver, an offer to do laundry, clean the house, run errands or do grocery shopping. You should feel free to call upon your friends who have pledged their support and availability.)

Matthew 11:28-30
Come to me, all you who are weary and burdened,
and I will give you rest. Take my yoke upon you and learn from me,
for I am gentle and humble in heart, and you will find rest
for your souls. For my yoke is easy and my burden is light.

Psalm 142:3a
When my spirit grows faint within me,
it is you who know my way.

Psalm 62:1
My soul finds rest in God alone; my salvation comes from him.

Isaiah 42:3a
A bruised reed he will not break, and a smoldering wick
he will not snuff out.

*O*my Savior, You invite us to come to You when we are weary and heavy burdened, and how well that describes our family today. My mind is sluggish, and I feel too tired to think. Making decisions about my health is such an effort. I believe Your promises, but right now I feel spiritually drained, and I have trouble grasping and holding on to them.

Weariness is also taking its toll on my body. I seem to just be going through the motions of living, rather than experiencing life. Lord, as I lie down to rest, please revive my entire being and give me energy to continue my walk in the Valley.

Let Your renewing power revive my weary family, as well. My illness is so difficult for them, and they too need to feel Your loving touch of refreshment.

Lord, thank you for friends who have given of their time to ease our burden. Please continue showing them when we need their help. Then when we have come through this crisis and our life is back to normal, make us aware of the needs of others, so we can come to their aid.

Let me now rest in You, content in knowing You are planning the way for me. You will always walk with me and my family, giving us strength to endure to the end. Indeed, You will carry us when we are too weary to take another step. I thank You for that assurance.

Weight Loss

$\mathcal{M}$any cancer patients experience weight loss as their bodies succumb to the wasting stage (cachexia) of their disease. This is very distressing. Even though they would like to eat more to keep their weight steady and fight their disease, they don't feel like eating at all. Interest in food wanes and fear of cancer overwhelms them.

Sometimes, as in my case, loss of weight may be due to increased exercise and a strict vegetarian diet. Whatever the cause, it produces the frustration of having a closet full of oversized clothing. Do we really have the money or energy to buy new clothing? Do we have a future in which to wear them? For me, thrift shops have solved my dilemma and I have come to enjoy what my son Dave calls "power shopping."

2 Corinthians 4:16
Therefore we do not lose heart. Though outwardly we are wasting away, yet inwardly we are being renewed day by day.

1 Timothy 6:6-8
But godliness with contentment is great gain. For we brought nothing into the world, and we can take nothing out of it. But if we have food and clothing, we will be content with that.

Psalm 139:14
I praise you because I am fearfully and wonderfully made; your works are wonderful, I know that full well.

$\mathcal{O}$ Lord God, how different my life has become. After years of checking for unwanted pounds, I now step onto the scales fearing they will show more weight loss. Even a slight gain gives me joy and reassurance. I humbly ask You to help me eat even when I have no appetite. Help me choose those foods which not only will be pleasant to my taste, but will also give my body nourishment and strength to fight my disease.

If my weight loss is due to the diet my doctor and I have chosen, or is caused by my long walks and increased exercise, then give me peace and the courage to continue these activities.

Forgive me for my frustration with having a closet full of clothing—all many sizes too large. I thank You for used clothing stores, because I can't make my clothes fit. Taking in seams or adding tucks or elastic just doesn't work anymore. I need new clothes. Bless the people who have made their clothing available at thrift shops.

Lord, help me see my new slim body with acceptance rather than fear that my disease is winning. Cancer never wins. You're in control, and You are never defeated, even if I die. Remind me that I am being inwardly renewed day by day.

So Lord, I give You all my concerns about my weight. Increase my desire, not only for physical food, but even more for the spiritual food You offer so freely (Isaiah 55:1-2). I pray for healing of my body and my spirit as I look to You to satisfy all my needs. Praise to You always.

Reflections & Prayers for God's Help When Experiencing These Feelings:

Abandonment
Anger
Anxiety
Discouragement
Fear
Fear of Death
Frustration
Guilt
Hopelessness
Loneliness
Pessimism, Negativism
Self-Centeredness
Worry

Abandonment

When struggling with cancer, our nerves may become frayed and emotions can be very fragile. This is especially true after surgery or during treatments. Feeling abandoned by loved ones is very hurtful and discouraging. Sometimes our perceptions may be accurate, but many times (probably most times) we misinterpret and overreact because of our vulnerability and unpredictable emotions. What we see as rejection may simply be their way of coping with the helplessness of watching us suffer.

In our distress we may also feel that God has left us, and this is the most devastating abandonment of all. We need to remind ourselves of the promises in scripture which tell us He will never leave us no matter what life may bring.

Psalm 22:1
My God, my God, why have you forsaken me? Why are you
so far from saving me, so far from the words of my groaning?

Deuteronomy 31:6b
The Lord your God goes with you;
he will never leave you nor forsake you.

James 4:8a
Come near to God and he will come near to you.

Psalm 9:18
But the needy will not always be forgotten,
nor the hope of the afflicted ever perish.

Psalm 37:27-28a
Turn from evil and do good; then you will dwell in the land forever.
For the Lord loves the just and will not forsake his faithful ones.

*O*Lord, You search me and know me; You are aware of my feelings of rejection, confusion and abandonment. I still need help and special consideration following my surgery (or chemotherapy, etc.), but because I am healing quickly and don't complain much, those close to me assume all is well. They seem to withdraw. Help me understand that this may be their way of coping with the stress and uncertainty of my illness. I realize my perceptions may be inaccurate, but if there is insensitivity in those around me, they probably are unaware of it. They would not hurt me intentionally. I forgive them now and remember the many ways in which they have blessed me in the past. I will not dwell on keeping a record of wrongs (1 Corinthians 13:5), real or perceived. Forgive me when my insensitivity has caused others to feel abandoned and rejected. Let me learn from this experience.

Lord, sometimes I feel abandoned by You, too. Forgive me for doubting Your promise that You will never leave me or forsake me.

Thank you for the care I receive from You and my loved ones. I dismiss any thoughts of abandonment, rejection or self-pity which may have taken root in my heart. I thank You that I have You; when I have You, I have everything!

Anger

For many people, the shock of a cancer diagnosis soon gives way to anger. This is not surprising since psychologists list anger as one of the steps in accepting life's blows and losses. This anger can be nebulous—not focused at anyone or anything in particular; at other times it is vented at doctors, nurses, family and friends. Usually these people are innocent bystanders who are trying to help. Much hurt is felt as they bear the brunt of this undeserved anger.

I suppose the ultimate anger is aimed at God Himself. Since we believe He holds our life in His hands, we feel He could have prevented us from getting this dreadful disease in the first place. It's all His fault! Similarly, He is able to heal, so we can blame Him for our continuing illness as well. If people battling cancer were totally honest, most probably they would have to admit to times of being angry at God.

Many aspects of my illness make no sense whatsoever. I wonder what God is doing to take control of the very confusing and distressing situations I continue to encounter. Sometimes this leads to anger.

This occurred when I was dealing with several cancer crises simultaneously, and in the midst of all that stress I found a lump in my breast. Since I had experienced a previous bout with breast cancer, this discovery was the last straw! My anger was aimed at God for allowing another lump to form at that time. How could He do this to me? Did He not know I already had too much stress? Where was He when I needed Him? As I allowed my anger to rise within my spirit (I really wanted to be angry!) I began to feel very far from God; in fact, I felt totally alienated. That was terrifying because I was faced with a dilemma: I felt my anger was justified, but I also knew I would lose all hope if I stayed far from the Lord. I realized my need to be close to my Heavenly Father as a little child. I remembered the Apostle Peter when he asked, "Lord to whom shall we go? You have the words of eternal life" (John 6:68). Knowing there was nowhere else to go for help, I chose to repent of my rebellious, angry attitude and let God be God. I did not understand the reason for my problems, but I believed God was able to deal with the situation more effectively than I could. It was a wonderful comfort to feel safe is His arms once again.

Many psychiatrists and Christian counselors suggest that anger at God is therapeutic, but there seem to be some pitfalls that need to be addressed. Anger as an emotion is not evil in itself; it's how we handle it that determines the sin. Telling God about anger leveled at Him (He already knows) may be all right; however, holding on to anger (at Him or anyone else) is dangerous, leading to a spirit of bitterness and hatred. Scripture warns us to never let the sun go down on our wrath; hence, all anger is to be short-lived. Prolonged anger definitely is not an emotion conducive to the very healing for which we strive. We must accept the truth of God's promises and trust Him to give us faith, courage and strength to continue our journey in the Valley.

Ephesians 4:26-27
In your anger do not sin: do not let the sun go down while you are still angry, and do not give the devil a foothold.

James 1:19
My dear brothers, take note of this: Everyone should be quick to listen, slow to speak and slow to become angry...

Proverbs 29:11
A fool gives full vent to his anger, but a wise man keeps himself under control.

Proverbs 29:22
An angry man stirs up dissension, and a hot-tempered one commits many sins.

Hebrews 12:15
See to it that no one misses the grace of God and that no bitter root grows up to cause trouble and defile many.

O Lord of my life, I feel so angry today. I'm angry at cancer for robbing me of so much. I also feel angry at the whole world, especially my family (spouse, doctors, nurses, friends, etc.) even though I realize they have done nothing wrong. I just want to be angry, and I don't understand that. Help me never to use my illness as an excuse for rudeness or verbally abusive behaviour. Please heal the hurts I have caused others when, in my anger and frustration, I have lashed out at them. Show me the root of this overwhelming emotion which is taking me captive today. I confess my sin and ask for Your forgiveness. Yes Lord, my wrath is aimed at You, too. It is beyond my comprehension why all these bad things are happening to me, and at times it seems as if You don't care. I know You could take away my suffering and even heal me. In my impatience I become angry when You choose to do otherwise. Forgive me and wash me, and I will be whiter than snow (Psalm 51:7).

Forgive me, too, when I envy those whose walk in life seems so much easier than my walk in the Valley. Sometimes I become angry because their life has not been disrupted by cancer as mine has. Help me remember that You love and care for me just as much as for them.

I ask You now to replace my anger with Your love and joy and that peace which passes all understanding (Philippians 4:7). Bless me once again with faith to believe that because You have a plan for my life, everything is under control. Lord, I do believe; help me overcome my unbelief (Mark 9:24).

Anxiety

*ancer has the notorious reputation of rendering its victims helpless and hopeless as it seeks to destroy their bodies. My most anxious times are during the hours leading up to surgery, treatments or medical consultations, or waiting for test results. Many times I feel a peace in my spirit that is not communicated to my physical senses. My heart insists on racing, and my stomach churns wildly in spite of the inner peace I feel. At other times both my spirit and my body succumb to anxiety. Then only repentance and looking anew to Jesus can lift me out of the pit. Guarding my thoughts against anxiety is easier for me than getting rid of it once I have allowed it to take root. Anxious emotions are very detrimental to the healing process, adversely affecting the immune system. God has good reason to caution us against entertaining anxious thoughts.

Dealing with the future is another sure way to increase my anxiety level. Hence, living one day at a time (in my "box for today") is extremely important. God is able to dispel my anxiety if I allow Him to renew my mind and heart.

Psalm 94:19
*When anxiety was great within me, your
consolation brought joy to my soul.*

I Peter 5:7
Cast all your anxiety on him because he cares for you.

Proverbs 12:25
*An anxious heart weighs a man down,
but a kind word cheers him up.*

O Lord, my anxious thoughts are overwhelming, making it

difficult for me to see You in this situation. By faith I believe You are near and will protect me, but I feel neither Your presence nor Your peace. Show me if I have willfully or unknowingly placed my feelings of anxiety over Your promises of peace. Have I chosen my anxious thoughts over You? Your precious blood can wash away all my sin, so I earnestly ask for Your forgiveness.

Please reveal Yourself to me once again, giving me the faith and strength to dismiss these anxious thoughts. I pray in the mighty name of Jesus for all my anxiety to flee and for peace to fill my whole being. You came to give me abundant life in all circumstances; I refuse to let anxiety rob me of that life. Show me how to experience fullness of life even in these disturbing days. You are victor over all evil, over my anxious thoughts and even cancer itself.

Discouragement
~≈~

When there are recurring bouts of cancer, discouragement is a very real threat to our peace. So often, just when we have the courage to hope our cancer is gone, a test result or newly discovered lump or symptom shatters our dreams. This, of course, means more tests, surgeries, biopsies or treatments.

For me this scenario has been repeated over and over again. However, I must never let discouragement rob me of my great hope in the Lord. In these situations I get much comfort from believing He already knows what is in store for me, providing for my needs and preparing my way. This shields me from the utter discouragement so many cancer patients experience daily. God always has ways to encourage me, even on the darkest days, but I must allow Him to do so, however and whenever He chooses.

Philippians 1:20
I eagerly expect and hope that I will in no way be ashamed,
but will have sufficient courage so that now as always
Christ will be exalted in my body, whether by life or by death.

Joshua 10:25a
Do not be afraid; do not be discouraged.
Be strong and courageous.

11 Corinthians 5:7
We live by faith, not by sight.

Psalm 31:24
Be strong and take heart, all you who hope in the Lord.

Lord, You tell me to be of good courage, but discouragement

hangs heavily around my whole being like a dismal, impenetrable cloud. I know and believe Your promises, but this new evidence of more cancer, just when I thought it was gone, is devastating. I am weary and discouraged and need a fresh touch from Your gracious hand. My spirit feels like a barren, arid desert where hope will never again dare to grow. Lord, I come to You for refreshing waters to flood my parched spirit so hope may once again take root.

Thank you that Your work in my life is not dependent on my feelings. Even now, while discouragement overwhelms me, You are already preparing my help.

Forgive me, my God, for my walking by sight rather than by faith. Bring to memory other times when discouragement sought to take me captive. There seemed to be no hope, no future, no way out, but indeed there was! You smiled on me, encouraged my heart and my spirit rejoiced once again. You are the Mighty God, able to dispel the darkest gloom and the deepest hopelessness.

Because of Your provision of help and salvation, I am confident in Your ability to do what is best for me. I have to understand neither how nor when You will accomplish that. I thank and praise You for who You are, as well as for what You are doing in my life.

Fear

*F*ear is an emotion cancer patients know all too well. Aside from the word 'cancer' itself, there are countless situations which produce fear: medical appointments, surgeries, biopsies, CAT scans, chemotherapy, radiation, test results, pain, the discovery of a new lump, etc.

Living in my "box for today," as well as singing praise songs and expressing my gratefulness to God, helps me to control these fearful thoughts. Nevertheless, there are times when fear almost paralyzes me. This is especially true while waiting for surgery or for a phone call or appointment which will reveal test results. At these times it takes all the grace available from the Lord to maintain my usual calm, peaceful frame of mind. Sharing my fears with my family and friends lightens my burden and allows them to pray for me. (At this writing, since a CAT scan is scheduled in two weeks, I am already asking God for His peace, grace and courage during the scan and the waiting period.)

When my fears have been conquered, I am very grateful to my Heavenly Father because only in Him am I able to overcome them.

Psalm 56:3
When I am afraid, I will trust in you.

Psalm 34:4
I sought the Lord, and he answered me;
he delivered me from all my fears.

Isaiah 43:1b
Fear not, for I have redeemed you;
I have summoned you by name; you are mine.

Isaiah 41:10

So do not fear, for I am with you; do not be dismayed,
for I am your God. I will strengthen you and help you;
I will uphold you with my righteous right hand.
(This is the key verse for my support group,
"CANSURVIVE, Days of Encouragement.")

O my God, You say, "Fear not!" but that is so difficult right now when my health situation is so overwhelming. I feel terrified and totally vulnerable. I can barely concentrate on anything other than my fearful thoughts which seem to explode in my head. Lord, I need Your peace and a fresh touch of Your love and courage.

(Make a list of all the cancer-related issues you fear and then pray about each one specifically. Also, share these concerns with people who will commit themselves to pray for you. I have always been very open with others when I have need of special prayer support.)

Fear of Death

*F*or most people, the word cancer evokes not only fear of the disease, but also fear of death. Everyone living in these last years of the twentieth century knows the dismal statistics which indicate that one in three people will contract cancer and many will die a painful, premature death. It is my conviction that our beliefs concerning death and an afterlife greatly influence the way in which we will cope with this insidious disease.

Scripture says, "Where, O death, is your victory? Where, O death, is your sting?" (1 Corinthians 15:55), but it also records the following words of the psalmist David: "My heart is in anguish within me; the terrors of death assail me. Fear and trembling have beset me; horror has overwhelmed me" (Psalm 55:4-5). Fear of death is a normal human reaction, involving fear of the unknown.

Since my hope and faith are in the Lord Jesus Christ and His salvation, my death will signify my crossing over from time into an eternity spent in God's presence. If I believe that (and I really do!) it would follow that I should have no fear of death. Yet when, at the age of fifty-one years, my oncologist predicted my death in about six months, I was afraid. In looking back, I think I feared the suffering prior to dying, more than death itself. I have known several people whose cancer deaths have been preceded by extreme pain, disfiguring surgeries, wasted limbs and bloated bellies. Memories of their suffering scare me, since I too am in a life-and-death battle against terminal cancer. By staying in my "box for today" I can avoid dwelling on those terrifying details. I want to live life as Merv's wife, and I hope to celebrate the weddings of our children and enjoy the miracle of being a grandma some day. Hence, my prayers for God's gift of healing and my vigorous war against cancer continue daily.

My holistic physician summed it up nicely. He said that although we both know the impossibility of extending my life one day beyond what our Lord has allotted me, we'll continue to do all we can to keep me healthy until that time.

Anita put it another way when someone, on hearing of my five-week 'heavy-duty detox' regime, asked if she didn't think her mom was overdoing it a bit. She replied, "We all know my mom is doing all she possibly can to get rid of her cancer. So if in the end she dies of cancer, it must be God's time for her to go. Then she will die in peace and we'll be okay." I thank God for helping me and my family conquer our fear of death, assuring us of His love and presence in life and in death. I can confidently say with St. Paul, "For to me, to live is Christ and to die is gain" (Philippians 1:21).

John 11:25-26
Jesus said to her, "I am the resurrection and the life.
He who believes in me will live, even though he dies; and whoever lives
and believes in me will never die. Do you believe this?"

Romans 14:8
If we live, we live to the Lord; and if we die, we die to the Lord.
So, whether we live or die, we belong to the Lord.

Psalm 18:4-6
The cords of death entangled me; the torrents of destruction
overwhelmed me. The cords of the grave coiled around me;
the snares of death confronted me. In my distress I called to the Lord; I
cried to my God for help. From his temple he heard my voice; my cry
came before him, into his ears.

Psalm 23:4, 6
Even though I walk through the valley of the shadow of death,
I will fear no evil, for you are with me; your rod and your staff, they
comfort me....Surely goodness and love will follow me all the days of
my life, and I will dwell in the house of the Lord forever.

Psalm 116:15
Precious in the sight of the Lord is the death of his saints.

O my precious Lord, You formed me in my mother's womb

and have cared for me throughout my life here on earth. As my death approaches, help me be faithful to You, trusting Your mercy and goodness to the end.

You tell me not to be afraid, but I do fear pain and suffering. If my time to go to be with You is near, please take me quickly so my suffering will soon end.

I beg for Your comfort and courage when I fear all the unknowns which death represents. Let me focus on what I do know: You will never leave me nor forsake me (Deuteronomy 31:6) and when I die I will spend eternity with You; I will dwell in Your house forever (Psalm 23:6). Also, You have gone to prepare a place for me (John 14:1-4). These promises give me comfort and peace and take away my fears.

I look forward to seeing You, my Savior and Lord. Into Your hands I commit my spirit.

Frustration

$\mathcal{M}$ost days I am able to take in stride my life in the Valley, but at times I feel frustrated and complaints begin to surface. My battle with cancer began in February 1989, and sometimes I lament that it has been "just too long!" Then I remind myself to be thankful for God's sustenance through all those years.

The complementary therapies I follow include time-consuming elements like juicing, rebounding (jumping on my mini trampoline to stimulate my lymph system), walking, coffee-retention enemas for bowel and liver detoxification, and getting enough rest. I become frustrated when there doesn't seem to be enough time to do it all, but I am very thankful to be alive.

I also stick to an organic vegetarian diet (I do eat organic meat and eggs occasionally, when my holistic physician agrees), but the high cost of such food, as well as the amount of time needed to prepare everything from scratch, is also very frustrating. (Convenience foods are forbidden.) However, once again I am reminded to be grateful for having the time and money required to follow the regime.

My paychecks have long ceased since I quit supply teaching on the advice of my doctor. Obviously we feel the lack of that money, but again I thank God for supplying all our needs and many of our wants through Merv's job.

The fact that most of my supplements, enzymes, etc., are not covered by our drug plan is very frustrating, particularly since the government would gladly have paid for chemotherapy, had I chosen that route, even though it would have been much more expensive and toxic. There definitely is a bureaucratic bias against alternative therapies, even when they work! Again I choose to be thankful instead of letting a spirit of frustration and bitterness take root.

In addition to using thankfulness as a "frustration buster," I find that laughing and joking about my experiences in the Valley also promotes a healthy, positive attitude. (My "coffee breaks" and rebounding have been the source of many family jokes!)

Considering the Israelites who spent forty years in the wilderness because of their murmuring, I try hard to nip frustration and complaining in the bud!

Philippians 4: 11b, 13,19

...for I have learned to be content whatever the circumstances....
I can do everything through him who gives me strength....
And my God will meet all your needs according to his
glorious riches in Christ Jesus.

Philippians 2:14

Do everything without complaining or arguing...

Heavenly Father, forgive me for murmuring and complaining. Help me be content in all circumstances. Teach me to accept my life in the Valley when my daily routines seem so different from those of healthy people. Many times I seem to be running behind schedule in the protocols I believe You have planned for me. However, with Your strength I know I will be able to continue.

Thank you for Your care during so many crises and setbacks. Without Your love I would surely perish in a sea of frustration and self-pity. Lord, please nudge my spirit to alert me whenever dissatisfaction and complaining are taking root in my mind. Thank you for showing me that in every frustrating circumstance, there is always something for which to be grateful.

I thank You now that, as my Provider, You will give me courage and the will to rise above my frustrations.

(List your frustrations and for each one find something for which to be thankful.)

_____

_____

_____

_____

_____

Guilt

I have never blamed myself for contracting cancer. My diet had always been nutritious with very little junk food, and I had never indulged in health-damaging habits like smoking, drinking or taking illicit drugs. Nonetheless, I have felt guilty at times. Because cancer has metastasized to many parts of my body, I have dealt with several life-threatening crises. I would never hurt my family intentionally, yet my illness does hurt them as they suffer with me and change their plans to accommodate me. This makes me feel guilty, even though I have not chosen these hard times for them. When I share my feelings of guilt for "putting you through this again," they don't understand. I suspect only those in my situation would really know how I feel.

I am grateful that my times of experiencing guilt are short-lived, because I feel so unworthy and just want to cry when dealing with these emotions. I always ask God to heal all my family's hurts, and I am thankful they never complain or put the blame on me. Instead they encourage me, and God removes my burden of guilt.

Psalm 38:4
My guilt has overwhelmed me like a burden too heavy to bear.

Hebrews 10:22
Let us draw near to God with a sincere heart in full assurance of faith, having our hearts sprinkled to cleanse us from a guilty conscience and having our bodies washed with pure water.

O Lord, I feel so guilty for once again being the cause of the trouble and stress my loved ones are feeling. It seems we often take one step forward and two steps backward as we walk in the Valley. Neither You nor my family condemn or blame me for my disease and yet I feel guilt and sadness in my spirit. I want so much to spare them from experiencing the hurts of another cancer crisis. Please shield them from frustration, hopelessness and discouragement as together we cope with and fight my disease.

Father, I am thankful for their care for me and their continuing support. Help me accept their words of encouragement and love so this crushing gloom will lift. I now renounce all feelings of guilt and ask You to protect my emotions.

Enfold us in Your loving arms as we prepare to support each other in the difficult days ahead. Bless our minds and bodies with the rest we so desperately need.

Hopelessness

Cancer is notorious for plunging its victims into a deep sea of hopelessness where all is dark. Many times I have struggled in that sea, crying out to Jesus to save me lest I drown. There is neither joy nor peace when hopeless emotions take us captive; we must fight hard to rid ourselves of this debilitating state of mind.

When I was given a "six-month death sentence" by my oncologist, I was absolutely overwhelmed by many negative emotions, but I believe hopelessness was the heaviest to bear. It would have robbed me of everything: my hope, peace, joy, health, plans to fight my disease, my future and indeed my life itself. Knowing it had the power to destroy us, Merv and I immediately sought prayer support from our friends. Initially, I was unable to pray; I just wept. But miraculously that hopelessness quickly lifted, and by God's grace I could again look to the future and plan it with hope in Him.

Since God is not the author of hopeless despair, He is able to give hope even in the face of death; hope in His mercy, grace and salvation. That hope, to a dying person who knows Jesus as his Savior, is eternal life, which assuredly is the ultimate hope.

Romans 15:13
May the God of hope fill you with all joy and peace as you trust in him, so that you may overflow with hope by the power of the Holy Spirit.

Psalm 62:5
Find rest, O my soul, in God alone; my hope comes from him.

Romans 12:12
Be joyful in hope, patient in affliction, faithful in prayer.

Psalm 147:11
The Lord delights in those who fear him,
who put their hope in his unfailing love.

Psalm 71:14
But as for me, I will always have hope;
I will praise you more and more.

Psalm 119:114
You are my refuge and my shield;
I have put my hope in your word.

O Lord of hope, have mercy on Your child. Right now, all is dark. Even though I know by faith that You are here, my sense of Your presence has left. I see no hope, no joy, no future…and my heart is about to break with sorrow. Since my test results (surgery, treatments, discouraging prognosis, death sentence, etc.) I am devoid of feelings. A dismal numbness has set in and has destroyed my will to continue on this journey. I have lost my will to live.

Lord, only You can restore that which hopelessness has stolen. No one else's words, care or love can lift my burdens, so I look to You, You alone, to heal my brokenness and breathe hope into my barren spirit. You are all I have and all that matters in this time of crisis. Help me have faith in Your plan for my future and in Your grace which is always sufficient for me to walk victoriously at all times. I pray, too, for Your blessing of renewed hope for my family as they seek to support and comfort me in my struggle. Lord, be our Hope and Strength in the days ahead. I love You and look to You.

Loneliness

*T*hose tiny, windowless cubicles where I have often disrobed and waited for an ultrasound or CAT scan may well be among the loneliest places on earth. When the wait is long (and it usually is), it seems as if no one even remembers that I am there. Perhaps I've been forgotten altogether! Claustrophobic tendencies and fear of the test can produce extreme feelings of loneliness and abandonment. To avoid these desperate emotions, I always focus on God's presence by praying while I wait.

Another place of loneliness is a darkened hospital room during the long hours of the night. Often the only sounds are the snores of a roommate fortunate enough to be sleeping or the groans of someone whose suffering is great. I have filled those lonely, sleepless hours with prayer and the silent singing of praise songs under my breath. (One hospital roommate had a delightful sense of humor which provided for many shared laughs. One night as I stared into the darkness, she also had awakened. Each of us tried to be very quiet so as not to disturb the other, whom we assumed to be asleep. Finally, realizing what was going on, she whispered, "You don't happen to have a deck of cards, do you? We could play a few rounds." We both burst out laughing and my sleepless loneliness vanished.)

Job loss due to illness produces the loneliness of staying at home while everyone else leaves for work. Since my days are filled with cancer-fighting routines and labor-intensive cooking, loneliness has never been a big problem. However, I do look forward to the time when Merv comes home each evening.

I suppose the times of greatest loneliness are in extreme suffering when people are waiting for death to release them from the frightful grip of cancer. Even though those patients may be surrounded by loved ones, their walk is a lonely one because no one quite understands the depth of their suffering. Ultimately, each person must face death alone.

I truly thank God that I can always call upon Him, so I am never really alone.

Hebrews 13:5b
…because God has said, "Never will I leave you;
never will I forsake you."

John 14:18
I will not leave you as orphans; I will come to you.

Romans 8:38-39
For I am convinced that neither death nor life, neither angels nor demons, neither the present nor the future, nor any powers, neither height nor depth, nor anything else in all creation, will be able to separate us from the love of God that is in Christ Jesus our Lord.

Revelation 3:20
Here I am! I stand at the door and knock. If anyone hears my voice and opens the door, I will come in and eat with him, and he with me.

*L*ord, I feel so lonely today. It seems as though everyone else has somewhere to go and things to do, but I am at home alone again. Cancer has radically changed my daily routines, in fact, my whole life. Help me cope with the loneliness these changes have brought.

Father, forgive me for complaining and feeling sorry for myself. Give me the courage I need to continue this lonely walk in the Valley.

Keep me mindful that I am never alone. You are always with me, supplying all my needs and blessing me with Your love and care. Show me how to fill my hours with constructive activities which will help me and bless those around me. Let my thoughts be focused on You rather than on my situation. You have planned my future and I trust the time spent alone will be for my good. Be my Teacher, Guide, Companion and Friend as I look to You for wisdom in dealing with my loneliness.

(Jot down your times of greatest loneliness. Pour out your heart to the Lord and ask Him to show you how to cope with these feelings and teach you how to use these times productively.)

Pessimism, Negativism

*I*t is my observation that there is a significant difference between discouragement and pessimism or negativism. A discouraged person may have lost hope, seeing no way out of his problems, but is open to the possibility of a solution. On the contrary, a pessimist refuses to even think there may be a way out. Cancer patients in the latter category respond to an encouraging report which indicates a good prognosis with words like, "So what! My cancer will just come back anyway!" That may well be a self-fulfilling prophecy if they remain in that frame of mind.

I am thankful to have been blessed with an optimistic personality. Usually my glass is "half full" instead of "half empty." This view of life has stood me in good stead throughout my years in the Valley.

Also, my personal faith in God, Who promises to care for us and cause everything to turn out for the good of those who love Him, has encouraged me to keep my heart and mind focused on Him rather than my health crises. Obviously this protects me from a health-destroying, negative attitude.

If you are battling these emotions, ask for God's help in overcoming them, and spend some quality time reflecting on the following Bible verses. There is scriptural and medical evidence indicating that a negative outlook is detrimental, while a life of thanksgiving and joyful hope in the Lord seems to promote better health and healing.

Proverbs 17:22
*A cheerful heart is good medicine, but a crushed
spirit dries up the bones.*

Psalm 42:5
*Why are you downcast, O my soul? Why so disturbed
within me? Put your hope in God, for I will yet praise him,
my Savior and my God.*

Philippians 4:8

Finally, brothers, whatever is true, whatever is noble, whatever is right, whatever is pure, whatever is lovely, whatever is admirable—if anything is excellent or praiseworthy—think about such things.

Romans 8:28

And we know that in all things God works for the good of those who love him, who have been called according to his purpose.

Psalm 100

(use this to lift your negative spirit)
Shout for joy to the Lord, all the earth. Worship the Lord with gladness; come before him with joyful songs. Know that the Lord is God. It is he who made us, and we are his; we are his people, the sheep of his pasture. Enter his gates with thanksgiving and his courts with praise; give thanks to him and praise his name. For the Lord is good and his love endures forever; his faithfulness continues through all generations.

O my Lord, I confess that I have become very negative about my cancer, myself and everyone around me. My life, in fact the whole world, looks black and hopeless; I feel angry and agitated. I know my pessimism is causing tension, confusion and pain in those who love and care for me. Forgive my unacceptable ways of dealing with my disease. Teach me the proper attitude conducive for healing, and help me to be more pleasant to those close to me.

My attempts at trying to cope without You have failed miserably. You desire that I give You complete control of my life and health, so I do that right now.

Let me walk forward in the Valley with faith and confidence in You, rejoicing in the knowledge that You are able to provide everything I need. Lord, I believe. Forgive my negative attitude of unbelief.

_____

_____

_____

_____

_____

Self-Centeredness

In the midst of battling cancer, we may become very self-centered. Our thoughts totally revolve around self and what is happening to that self, both physically and emotionally. My joy, peace and courage quickly vanish when my attention is focused inward on me and my disease. Dwelling on my problems has the power to rob me of many blessings God desires for me. It also blinds me to the needs of others.

One of the most rewarding aspects of my life is my time spent encouraging others in their walk in the Valley. Praying for them and helping them in their struggles easily shifts my focus from my concerns to theirs.

Focusing my thoughts on God and His blessings also turns my attention away from my battle with cancer. My problems seem so small when I truly let Him be in control, knowing that His power is greater than anything I will ever encounter in the Valley. This is much more health-producing than dwelling on "poor me" and feeling hard done by.

Philippians 2:3-4
Do nothing out of selfish ambition or vain conceit, but in humility consider others better than yourselves. Each of you should look not only to your own interests, but also to the interests of others.

1 Corinthians 13:4-5
Love is patient, love is kind. It does not envy, it does not boast, it is not proud. It is not rude, it is not self-seeking, it is not easily angered, it keeps no record of wrongs.

2 Corinthians 5:15
And he died for all, that those who live should no longer live for themselves but for him who died for them and was raised again.

O Lord, it seems that cancer has become my whole focus. However, the more my thoughts dwell on me and my illness, the more my thoughts are farther from You and Your promises.

My body is being ravaged by a deadly disease, but it is more important that I allow You to renew me inwardly. Help me to keep my mind on You and Your work of grace and salvation, rather than on my illness which is interfering with my life and agenda.

Show me, in the midst of all my turmoil, when others need my attention and kind words. I will miss these opportunities as long as my concern is for me only. Forgive me for thinking my needs are somehow greater than those of others, or that my disease is worse. O God, alert my spirit the instant I allow selfish thoughts to creep into my mind.

I rejoice in what You are doing in me and for me. I believe You are all Wisdom, so as the Great Physician, You are able to care for me. Help me extend loving care to others so they, too, may know You as their Healer.

Thank you for having everything under control. You are my Savior.

Worry

When living with cancer, life is filled with tests, biopsies, treatments, surgeries, etc. These are always followed by tense periods of waiting for results. During these times worry has to be battled daily, sometimes even minute by minute. God promises His grace and aid for all of life's experiences, but nowhere does He make such promises for when we worry. Therefore, I have come to believe that worrying about a situation is always much worse than the real experience.

For instance, I would have thought being given a "death sentence" would destroy me. When that happened, God's peace soon dispelled my anxiety. I could not have imagined that beforehand. Another great fear was cancer metastases in a major organ. However, when a CAT scan in June 1996 revealed metastatic kidney cancer tumors in my liver and renal bed, as well as swollen peri-pancreatic lymph nodes, God's grace was once again sufficient for the situation. I strive to always stay in my "box for today" for He will take care of tomorrow.

Physiology has shown that anxiety or worry greatly debilitates our immune system, thus hindering our healing. God's caution against worrying is well worth heeding.

We are invited to rest in Him, trusting in His ability and promise to care for us. He will take care of the future.

Psalm 37:8b
Do not fret—it leads only to evil.

Matthew 6:34
Therefore do not worry about tomorrow, for tomorrow will worry about itself. Each day has enough trouble of its own.

Matthew 6:27
Who of you by worrying can add a single hour to his life?

O dearest Lord, gaining victory over worry is so difficult these days. The lab report (biopsy, etc.) will either give me a new lease on life or another death sentence. Is it possible to put all my worries aside? Your Word tells me to do so, therefore it must be possible with Your help.

My mind races ahead, trying to imagine the ramifications of different results. Help me, O God, to control these renegade thoughts and take them to the foot of Your cross.

Help me stay in my "box for today." I have so much for which to thank You: my family, home, food, clothing, friends, church, good doctors, etc. (Spend time on these and other blessings you have received. A spirit of gratitude can dispel worry.)

Above all, I thank You for sending Jesus to redeem me by His shed blood on the cross. Let me feel His love this day. Words are inadequate to describe my gratitude in knowing my Redeemer lives and His promises are true, no matter how dismal my circumstances may be.

It gives me great comfort that You already know my prognosis, so in faith I believe You are making provisions for me. All my needs will be met because You are my Provider.

I thank You, too, for inviting me to take this heavy burden of worry and uncertainty off my shoulders and put it on Yours. I am grateful that You give me freedom and joy to live each day to the fullest, even during these days of waiting. The peace I now feel is the "peace that passes all understanding" (Philippians 4:7). You are a God of miracles, and I trust You, no matter what, for You are bigger than any cancer crisis. My life is held securely in Your hands.

Reflections & Prayers
When in Need of:

Ability to Enjoy the Present Moment
(living one day at a time)
Faith
Healing
Joy
Patience
Peace
Protection from Side Effects
Staying in My "Box for Today"
Strength to Carry On
Wisdom

Ability to Enjoy
the Present Moment
(living one day at a time)

Worries concerning the future can rob cancer patients of many golden opportunities for creating pleasant memories. God taught me several years ago to stay in my "box for today," and I have found that when I deal with the present only, the blessings of each day are easier to recognize and enjoy. A visit or letter from a friend, an encouraging medical appointment, a loving word from my husband or children, even a little bird singing outside my window all bring me much joy in spite of my ongoing health problems. Negative emotions such as self-pity or worry would completely block out these little pleasures.

Similarly, when focusing my attention on the future and what I hope to do when I am rid of cancer, I miss living each day to the fullest. I try to appreciate all the little graces God gives me, remembering that the joys and opportunities of this day will be gone forever if I do not see them and respond with gratitude.

I also avoid the "if only" syndrome: "If only I did not have cancer, then I would..." "If only I didn't need chemotherapy, then I would..." "If only I didn't need surgery, then I would..." "If only" can become the ultimate cop-out for a cancer patient.

Also, the needs of those around me will go unnoticed if my mind is somewhere other than the present moment. I don't want my illness to become an excuse for overlooking their needs.

In some of my worst crises, enjoying the present moment has been very difficult if not impossible, but through it all I have learned that God's provision is moment by moment, day by day. That is how I must live my life, savoring the blessings as I encounter them each day in my journey in the Valley.

Psalm 118:24
This is the day the Lord has made; let us rejoice and be glad in it.

Psalm 90:12
Teach us to number our days aright,
that we may gain a heart of wisdom.

Psalm 139:16b
All the days ordained for me were written in your
book before one of them came to be.

O my Father, help me live in my "box for today." I try so hard, but still I get anxious as questions about my future explode in my mind. "Will I ever be rid of my disease?" "How long will my time in the Valley continue?" "Will I die a painful cancer death?" I am grateful You know the answers to my questions and so I need not worry about them. Let me never forget that fretting is sin. Help me see all the blessings You are giving me today. Anxiety makes me overlook them, and I begin to think that nothing good ever happens to me. Then I sink into the pit of self-pity. Forgive me for those thoughts which have the power to destroy me.

Give me the grace to see each day, indeed each moment, as a wonderful gift from You to be received with joy and gratitude. Open my eyes to see the needs of my family and friends and show me how I can reach out and be a blessing to them. Remind me that even though I do not understand why my problems continue, You always are in control, planning my future. Only when I truly believe this will I be able to live each day to the fullest. You have promised abundant life to Your followers, and I depend entirely on You to help me receive that life as I continue my journey in the Valley, one day at a time.

Faith

Scripture and my own experiences have taught me that faith is essential to live victoriously while battling cancer. My personal faith is in the triune God—Father, Son (Jesus Christ, my Savior) and Holy Spirit—and I trust in His mercy, grace and healing as He involves Himself in my daily struggles. I consecrate my life to Him.

However, there are times when my cancer crises make no sense and I need to ask for a stronger faith in God's goodness, wisdom and faithfulness. Faith comes easily when life is going well, but it is in the difficult times that my faith is tried, tested and refined as gold in the refiner's fire. When the fire is hot and my trials seem unbearable, I need a fresh touch of faith from the Lord to continue my perilous journey in the Valley. Faith is a gift from Him, and I thank Him for hearing and answering my prayers when I ask for it.

Shortly after a CAT scan in June 1996 revealed that cancer had spread to my liver, renal bed and peri-pancreatic lymph nodes, Merv and I were worshipping with some friends in their "vacation church." The sermon was based on the little song "Jesus Loves Me." Then the congregation was invited to come up to the altar and sing that song as a reaffirmation of faith in the Lord Jesus. It was very moving and it seemed to me that Jesus was asking, "Do you still love me in spite of that CAT scan?" I started to weep and felt my doubts being washed away as my faith was strengthened. I knew I could tell Him I still loved Him, probably more than ever before. That morning I received a profound faith boost to help me through the days ahead. My health problems are always far less distressing when I have enough faith to put my life entirely in God's hands, believing He will do what is best for me.

Faith also banishes my fear of dying, for I know death is only a step into an eternity which I will spend with my Lord. Without faith I would surely be consumed by doubt, depression, terror and hopelessness.

Hebrews 11:1
*Now faith is being sure of what we hope
for and certain of what we do not see.*

2 Corinthians 5:7
We live by faith, not by sight.

1 Peter 1:6-9
*In this you greatly rejoice, though now for a little
while you may have had to suffer grief in all kinds of trials.
These have come so that your faith—of greater worth
than gold, which perishes even though refined by fire—
may be proved genuine and may result in praise, glory
and honor when Jesus Christ is revealed. Though you have
not seen him, you love him; and even though you do not
see him now, you believe in him and are filled with an
inexpressible and glorious joy, for you are receiving
the goal of your faith, the salvation of your souls.*

Merciful Father, thank you for Your gift of faith. Help me as well as my loved ones to cling to it, no matter what is happening around us. Teach us to walk by faith rather than by sight. If I concentrate on what I see, despair quickly robs me of my faith in You. Forgive me when I choose to walk by sight, shutting You out because I do not understand what You are doing in my life.

Lord, I beg You to strengthen my faith in Your love, compassion, healing, faithfulness and salvation. Let me trust Your plans for my future, believing You will never leave me nor forsake me.

Also give me faith in Your healing power, so I will be prepared to receive whatever healing You would offer me. Take my weak, faltering faith and make it strong. Lord, I believe. Help my unbelief!

Healing

Healing is the burning desire and dream of most cancer patients. It is also one of the most soul-searching faith issues with which we wrestle. There are many around us who are absolutely convinced that God never heals today; that was only for biblical times. There are others just as adamant that not only does God still heal, but one need only have the faith to claim it to be totally healed. Therefore, lack of healing simply indicates a lack of faith. What a burden to load on a suffering believer!

I believe with my whole heart that God still performs miracles, totally healing some people by His supernatural power alone or through medical procedures. His healing power has been demonstrated many times in my life and that of my family and friends. However, I cannot deny having known several very devout Christians who died of cancer, even though they knew and loved the Lord and believed the scriptures about healing. How does one reconcile their deaths with the following scripture verses: *He forgives all my sins and heals all my diseases.* (Psalms 103:3)....*and by His wounds we are healed* (Isaiah 53:5). *Ask and it will be given....For whoever asks receives* (Matthew 7:7-8). *You do not have, because you do not ask God* (James 4:2b). *Daughter, your faith has healed you. Go in peace* (Luke 8:48).

Having wrestled with this while struggling with recurring, life-threatening cancer crises since 1989, I have come to the conclusion that God will heal me in His own time and manner. The choice is His. Moreover, I need not fear death. St. Paul saw dying as gain (Philippians 1:21). For the believer, death truly is the ultimate healing!

I realize that faith is essential, but I am also convinced there is a big difference between faith and presumption. Even though I continue to fight my disease vigorously and pray for healing, my greatest desire is to glorify God and be used by Him—with or without cancer.

Medically speaking, I should have died long ago; that I have not in itself can be called a miraculous healing. Still, my body produces many malignant tumors (metastases of kidney cancer), so claiming a total healing would be very misleading, in fact, dishonest.

Whatever healing God offers, whether physical, spiritual or emotional, I am very eager to receive. Although I have been anointed with oil many times and I pray daily for healing, I do not demand it. I strive to live each day to the fullest, always thanking God for His love and care, confident that His will for me is the very best.

James 5:14-15
Is any one of you sick? He should call the elders of the church
to pray over him and anoint him with oil in the name of the Lord.
And the prayer offered in faith will make the sick person well;
the Lord will raise him up. If he has sinned, he will be forgiven.

Matthew 14:14
When Jesus landed and saw a large crowd,
he had compassion on them and healed their sick.

Mark 3:10
For he had healed many, so that those with diseases
were pushing forward to touch him.

Psalm 103:2-3
Praise the Lord, O my soul, and forget not all his benefits—who
forgives all your sins and heals all your diseases.

O my beloved Father, I pray that You would touch me and heal me of this dreadful disease. Your Word tells me that Jesus healed many people as He walked on the earth. Since He is the same yesterday, today and forever (Hebrews 13:8), I trust that He can do the same for me today. You also tell me I will receive whatever I ask in Jesus' name (Matthew 7:8). I do believe You are able to heal me; yet my cancer continues to spread throughout my body. Search my heart and show me if there is any sin or unbelief blocking my healing. Forgive me and give me a fresh supply of faith if You find me lacking. Lord, I believe; help me overcome my unbelief (Mark 9:24).

Protect me from the discouragement brought by people who do not believe that You heal today. Also protect me from the guilt and confusion caused by those who insinuate I have a great lack of faith. Their way of dealing with disease would be to demand healing and claim it. Show me the truth and balance between these two extremes.

Lord, no matter how great my suffering, I believe You have planned my future in love, so I will receive with gratitude whatever healing You provide for me. Thank you for the healing, comfort, love and peace You have already given as You have walked with me and my family in the Valley. I am truly grateful for all Your mercies, and I put my life into Your hands once more.

Heal me, O Lord, and I will be healed; save me and I will be saved, for You are the One I praise (Jeremiah 17:14). Thank you, my precious Savior. Help me keep my eyes on You, the Healer, rather than on the healing which I sincerely desire.

Joy

~~~

*F*or many cancer patients joy is no longer part of their daily experience. Their furrowed brows and deep sighs attest to this fact.

Because God has blessed me with much joy, people often ask, "How can you be so happy when you have terminal cancer?" Even though I know my joy is a gracious gift from the Lord, I guard my heart zealously. When joy vanishes due to emotions controlled by anger, impatience or fear, I immediately confess my sin to God, asking Him to restore to me the joy of my salvation (Psalm 51:12).

Many times I force myself to sing praise songs to dispel the gloom. To fight my disease I need all the strength which the joy of the Lord provides. My immune system will benefit from this joy as it seeks to restore my body to full health by destroying all my cancer cells.

Psalm 86:3-4
Have mercy on me, O Lord, for I call to you
all day long. Bring joy to your servant, for to you,
O Lord, I lift up my soul.

Nehemiah 8:10b
...for the joy of the Lord is your strength.

Romans 15:13
May the God of hope fill you with all joy and peace as you
trust in him, so that you may overflow with hope
by the power of the Holy Spirit.

*O*my Lord, I confess that I have allowed frustration, discouragement, confusion and fear to replace my joy. Truly, I see nothing happy in my life today, just more pain and uncertainty as my cancer spreads. And yet many times Your Word promises us joy—full joy.

Have You abandoned me? Am I beyond Your gift of joy today? My mind knows the answers, but my heart cries out, "My joy has departed; will it ever come back?" Help me trust that even in severe crises, I still can experience joy in Your presence, mercy, forgiveness and, most of all, in Your free gift of salvation. Remind me to keep my eyes fixed on You so my joy will return. I desire to take joy in Your love and care for me right now. Through all my struggles You have been faithful, and I trust in Your continuing sustenance and provision. By faith I ask You to forgive me and fill me once again with Your joy. Then let me pass that joy on to those I meet today.

Patience

*E*ven though patience is a fruit of the Spirit (Galatians 5:22), many aspects of living with cancer can produce a state of mind driven by impatience. Some of my waiting periods for tests have been five weeks, with an additional two weeks for the results. Since this information deals with life and death issues, my patience wears thin. Time seems to drag as I try to imagine why the wait is so long.

My patience was tried during the five weeks of radiation treatments following my surgery for breast cancer. Since I was very eager to get on with my life as a substitute teacher, those weeks seemed to pass so slowly. I just wanted the treatments behind me.

At times my impatience is aimed at God. His timing and mine are hardly ever the same, but I trust His way is best. My goal is to spend more time patiently waiting for Him and allowing Him to answer my prayers in His time.

I have had to learn to be patient with myself (or rather, my body). Being a very active, energetic person, I easily become impatient when I don't recuperate as quickly as I had hoped. This is especially true after general anesthesia. I feel lethargic and listless for quite some time. (It took many weeks of sitting in my rocking chair after my kidney surgery until I had any ambition to do anything.) This is very difficult considering my "get-up-and-go" mentality.

Living in my "box for today" helps me cope in these situations. When I deal with frustrations as they confront me, one day at a time, patience is more attainable. Trying to deal with tomorrow's problems is sure to produce impatient thoughts.

Also, a spirit of gratefulness helps to dispel my impatience. If I stop murmuring long enough to count my blessings, I feel calm, knowing that God has everything under control.

Galatians 5:22-23a
But the fruit of the Spirit is love, joy, peace, patience, kindness, goodness, faithfulness, gentleness and self-control.

Psalm 40:1
I waited patiently for the Lord; he turned to me and heard my cry.

Romans 12:12
Be joyful in hope, patient in affliction, faithful in prayer.

Psalm 27:14
Wait for the Lord; be strong and take heart and wait for the Lord.

O my Father, I confess my feelings of impatience as I again await my tests (test results, etc.). Please forgive me when, in my impatience and complaining, I neglect to thank You for Your countless blessings. Help me live each of these days of waiting to the fullest.

Forgive me, too, when I allow impatient thoughts to create stress for my family and friends. Let me never take out my frustrations and impatience on them. They have been a wonderful support network during my crises, and I am grateful for their care. Show me when my health situation blinds me from seeing their needs. Let me be a blessing to them even now as I struggle to overcome these overwhelming feelings of impatience.

And so, Lord, I ask for Your help today. Help me keep my eyes on You as I allow Your peace to calm my agitated, impatient spirit.

Peace

*P*eace is promised to us by our loving Heavenly Father. At times both peace and trust are very illusive, staying just beyond our grasp. I find that these times call for simply resting in Jesus instead of striving to produce peace within. A child in a loving parent's arms has perfect trust and perfect peace. He feels safe while in those arms. So too, we can avail ourselves of peace by totally relinquishing all our concerns and resting in our Lord's arms.

At times this may truly be impossible but God has often used ordinary events, such as a phone call at just the right time, a beautiful sight, the singing of a bird or an appropriate scripture verse, to restore my peace. His ways of blessing us are infinite, and His timing always is perfect. We are His children, whom He dearly loves and cares for. His desire is that we experience His awesome peace in all circumstances. We need to desire it, too.

Isaiah 26:3
You will keep in perfect peace him whose mind is steadfast,
because he trusts in you.

Philippians 4:6-7
Do not be anxious about anything, but in everything, by prayer and
petition, with thanksgiving, present your requests to God.
And the peace of God, which transcends all understanding,
will guard your hearts and your minds in Christ Jesus.

Proverbs 14:30
A heart at peace gives life to the body, but envy rots the bones.

Psalm 29:11
The Lord gives strength to his people,
the Lord blesses his people with peace.

O God of peace, I beg for Your touch today. The peace I usually experience has departed, leaving an aching void which is fast filling with fear and anxiety. Show me what is blocking Your peace which I desire. Is my mind focused on my disease rather than on You? Have I put my trust in doctors and medical procedures rather than in Your healing power? Lord, forgive me if You find these sins in me. Forgive me, too, when I purposely block the flow of Your peace with rebellious, angry and impatient thoughts. I repent and ask You to wash me clean.

Help me guard my mind, and show me the perfect way which is trusting You as a little child. Let me humble myself, casting all my anxieties on You, for You care for me (1 Peter 5:7). Teach me to keep my mind on You, for You alone can give that perfect peace which I so desperately need. Let me, like St. Paul, think on things true, noble, right, pure, lovely, admirable, excellent or praiseworthy (Philippians 4:8). So many of my experiences in dealing with cancer are just the opposite. Only You can help me replace my negative, fearful thoughts with positive, God-centered ones so Your promised peace will flow in my spirit once again.

Thank you, Lord, for giving me faith to believe that Your peace will return.

Protection from Side Effects

Cancer tests and treatments have side effects ranging from minimal to life threatening. I ask many questions and do my own research before consenting to such procedures. For example, my refusal of bone scans was based on the fact that I considered the radioactive dye invasive. On questioning my oncologist, it became clear that nothing could be done to heal my bones if lesions were detected by the scan. After much prayer, I concluded that the test would do more harm than good to my weakened immune system. I also refused chemotherapy when it was offered, because I had read of its ineffectiveness as a kidney cancer treatment. In contrast, the benefits of the radiotherapy treatments for breast cancer seemed to outweigh the dangers.

These are tough decisions faced by all cancer patients. However, with God's wisdom we can confidently make the proper choices. Remember, the choice is yours! Whenever choosing invasive therapies or tests, I always pray for God's protection from adverse side effects.

Psalm 16:1
Keep me safe, O God, for in you I take refuge.

Psalm 32:7
You are my hiding place; you will protect me from trouble and surround me with songs of deliverance.

Psalm 5:11
But let all who take refuge in you be glad; let them ever sing for joy. Spread your protection over them, that those who love your name may rejoice in you.

Psalm 91:4
He will cover you with his feathers, and under his wings you will find refuge; his faithfulness will be your shield and rampart.

O Lord, I have chosen radiation treatments (chemotherapy, surgery, biopsy, etc.) and I fear the harm it can cause to my body and immune system. However, believing this is Your will for me, I trust in Your protection. As my cancer cells are attacked, killed or removed by this procedure, I pray that my healthy ones will remain undamaged. O God, let my cancerous cells be totally destroyed throughout my body so this disease will be conquered. If my normal cells are affected, I pray for Your rejuvenation and healing. Show me how to eat and live to give my body the very best chance of recovery. Grant me patience in all of this. Help me always to look to You as I go through this new crisis. Thank you for being with me even in my pain. Please sustain and comfort my family as they watch my suffering. Give them peace and remove their fears so they will be able to support and care for me when necessary. Walk with all of us now and protect us from all harm.

Staying in My "Box for Today"

*L*iving in my "box for today" is one of my key strategies for coping with ongoing cancer crises. Since I believe God taught me this concept, I strive diligently to live each day in my box, leaving the future in His capable hands.

In December 1991 (almost three years after my battle with kidney cancer began) I was informed after surgery that the lump which had been removed from my breast was malignant. I had breast cancer! That this was a different kind of cancer was very distressing, but I was assured it was much preferable to a return of my kidney cancer.

On the day following my lumpectomy, while contemplating my new health crisis, I experienced what I believe was a vision from the Lord. I saw a calendar page. Instead of lines forming squares to mark the days, there were walls creating boxes around each day. Then I heard the words, "You must not go out of your box for today." Obviously it meant I should live one day at a time without worrying about the future. This has had a lasting effect on our family, and we often remind each other to stay in our "box for today" when we begin worrying about the future.

Staying in my box while awaiting surgery, tests or lab results is especially important. I repeatedly tell myself, "It's not in my box for today," and with God's help I usually succeed in conquering my fearful thoughts. I have thanked Him many times for giving me this visual aid to help me cope with my disease.

2 Corinthians 10:5
*We demolish arguments and every pretension that sets itself
up against the knowledge of God, and we take captive every
thought to make it obedient to Christ.*

Matthew 6:34
Therefore do not worry about tomorrow,

for tomorrow will worry about itself.
Each day has enough trouble of its own.

Matthew 6:27
Who of you by worrying can add a single hour to his life?

Psalm 139:16b
All the days ordained for me were written in
your book before one of them came to be.

O Heavenly Father, teach me to live in my "box for today." Your Word indicates that all my days were ordained by You, so I believe You have a plan for my life this day. Help me take all my thoughts captive and renounce those which deal with the concerns of tomorrow. Right now that is very difficult. I desperately need Your help lest I become overwhelmed with fear, anxiety and utter hopelessness.

Remind me of Your grace which is always sufficient for today. Tomorrow I will receive a fresh supply of mercy, grace and strength from Your hand.

Forgive me for choosing to look at my problems rather than to You. I repent and ask You to teach me once again to live one day at a time. You are my only hope, and You alone are able to deliver me from my fears concerning the future. Bless me as I look to You, trusting in Your care, no matter what lies ahead. Thank you for today.

Strength to Carry On

*T*here have been times in my battle against cancer when I have felt like giving up. The strength to carry on seemed to have evaporated, and I was tempted to just sit back and let cancer have its way with me. These feelings usually surface when a test or biopsy reveals new metastatic tumors. At these times the support and encouragement of family and friends is vital. They are like coaches, urging me, the runner, to persevere to the finish line. I am very grateful for their care and loving concern. I also thank God for those doctors who dare to speak encouragement, life and faith, even when the prognosis is dismal.

Psalm 23 is most helpful, especially the words, "He restores my soul." When I take my eyes off my problems and focus on my Shepherd, my soul is indeed restored, and the strength to continue my perilous journey in the Valley is supplied. Without God's help this would be impossible.

Negative emotions, such as fear, worry, anger and despair, greatly decrease my will to continue the fight. At the first signs of such feelings, I seek God's help to control and get rid of them. He is always faithful in coming to my aid whenever I call, supplying all my needs. It is by His infinite grace that I continue to receive the strength to carry on in my fight with cancer.

Psalm 18:1-2a
I love you, O Lord, my strength. The Lord is my rock,
my fortress and my deliverer; my God is my rock,
in whom I take refuge.

Psalm 105:4
Look to the Lord and his strength;
seek his face always.

2 Corinthians 12:9a
But he said to me, "My grace is sufficient for you,
for my power is made perfect in weakness."

James 1:12
Blessed is the man who perseveres under trial,
because when he has stood the test, he will receive the
crown of life that God has promised to those who love him.

2 Corinthians 4:17-18
For our light and momentary troubles are achieving
for us an eternal glory that far outweighs them all.
So we fix our eyes not on what is seen, but on what is unseen.
For what is seen is temporary, but what is unseen is eternal.

My Lord and my God, I am too weary and discouraged to persevere any longer. In fact, I don't know how I'll get through this day. I definitely need a fresh touch from You right now. Bring to my memory all the other times I felt like giving up, and You picked me up and carried me over the rough and treacherous road that lay ahead. My strength and courage came back when I looked to You and allowed You to carry me. You sent people who prayed for me and brought me words of love and encouragement. Lord, I ask for those blessings today.

Forgive me for taking Your countless mercies for granted. Forgive me too for giving more thought to my problems than to You and Your provisions.

Give me faith to believe You still are planning my future, day by day, in love. Help me to trust in Your strength when I feel so weak.

Thank you for assuring me that I will be able to persevere and push ahead in this battle when I receive the strength You have promised. I rest in You now.

Wisdom

When fighting cancer, there are so many decisions to be made. Doctors and natural healthcare practitioners, as well as family and friends, should have input, but the final decision must be made by the patient. What a heavy burden and responsibility! This has been especially true for me at those times when I have rejected toxic oncological therapies in favor of less toxic (mostly non-toxic) complementary protocols. It is most frightening to refuse the very treatments which are chosen by most other people. However, after much prayer, Merv and I always have peace when I make these life and death decisions. Without God's wisdom and strength, I could not make such critical choices. Since each person and each case is different, it is of the utmost importance that each cancer patient makes his own decisions in light of God's will for him at that particular time.

James 1:5
If any of you lacks wisdom, he should ask God,
who gives generously to all without finding fault,
and it will be given to him.

Psalm 111:10
The fear of the Lord is the beginning of wisdom;
all who follow his precepts have good understanding.

Psalm 32:8
I will instruct you and teach you in the way you should go;
I will counsel you and watch over you.

Proverbs 2:6
For the Lord gives wisdom, and from
his mouth come knowledge and understanding.

O Lord, I am overwhelmed and feel as if I am on "information overload." Somehow I have to sift through everything I have been told or have read and then come to some conclusions. Give me clarity of mind. Some suggestions are beyond my understanding, due to my insufficient medical knowledge; other pieces of information clearly contradict each other. I know that my choices can either lead to more sickness and even death, or to healing and life. This is an awesomely frightening responsibility, so I need Your wisdom as I contemplate the options before me.

I rebel at the thought of the toxicity and severe side effects of chemotherapy and radiation, but if that is Your will for me I will bear the suffering. However, if through diet, exercise, vitamins and other natural routines, You desire to strengthen my immune system so it can fight cancer, I would gladly persevere in following that protocol. Lord, only You know how my body will react, and only You know what Your plan for my life really is. This You have known since my conception (Psalm 139:16b). Show me Your battle plan for me as I fight my disease. Guide me through this medical maze, and enable me to put my fears and preconceived ideas aside so they will not block my ability to hear You. Thank you for having the answers I need. I ask now for courage to obey Your voice. Come Lord Jesus, my Great Physician. I pray for Your healing power in whatever treatment You choose for me.

Reflections & Prayers of Thanksgiving for These Blessings:

Anniversaries, Birthdays, Holidays
Cancer Milestones
Caring, Competent Doctors
Everyday Blessings and Experiences
Financial Sufficiency
God's Promises
Good Health, Good Days
Good Prognoses (test results, etc.)
Joy
Laughter, A Good Sense of Humor
Peace
Seasonal Changes

Anniversaries, Birthdays, Holidays

The quality and tone of family celebrations are very much affected by cancer. They can be very joyous, painfully tense or profoundly sad, depending on the health status of the cancer patient. For me, my fiftieth birthday was very special and I remember it fondly. I was forty-five when first diagnosed; in the next five years I also contracted breast cancer and kidney cancer metastases. When I was told that only one to two per cent of people with that kind of metastases survive for five years, I obviously thought my time was short. Hence, the surprise party Merv and the kids planned was a very wonderful celebration. The guests were friends who had faithfully prayed for me.

Our twenty-fifth wedding anniversary was another joyous landmark, since by then we had been in the Valley for over three years. However, due to the stress of my health crises, it was a very quiet time of thanksgiving. Many metastases and a death sentence later, we celebrated our thirtieth anniversay in August of 1997! I find that, in all our celebrations, I catch myself wondering if "I'll be here next year," but I refuse to dwell on those thoughts.

Cancer crises often recur at the same time of year, because tests and consultations are scheduled at six- and twelve-month intervals. One friend confided that she hated spring. Almost all of her periods of intense cancer suffering took place at the very time when everyone else was enjoying the beautiful outdoors.

For our family it is the Christmas season which floods our minds with tense memories of previous cancer crises. The joy and excitement of putting up our tree is tempered by a sense of foreboding. In fact, when we had finished decorating our tree last year, I said to my daughter Anita how wonderful it was that there were no imminent crises for a change. She replied, "Yes, but I feel as if I'm just waiting for the other shoe to drop." Dismantling the tree brings to memory the year I packed every ball and trinket especially carefully, thinking

I would no longer be alive to unpack them the next Christmas.

While it would probably be emotionally beneficial to discuss these memories, for some reason we usually try to bury them. Perhaps we don't want to remind each other of those hard times. How foolish; we are all thinking of them anyway.

In all of these emotionally charged occasions, I spend much time thanking God for the opportunity of enjoying another birthday (Christmas, anniversary, etc.). I try to eagerly anticipate and prepare for each special event. We continue long-range planning in spite of my terminal illness. We never put our lives on hold because of cancer. Living in gratitude to our Lord makes this possible, and we do feel very blessed as we celebrate important dates in our family.

Ecclesiastes 3:4
...a time to weep and a time to laugh,
a time to mourn and a time to dance...

Psalm 118:24
This is the day the Lord has made;
let us rejoice and be glad in it.

Philippians 4:4
Rejoice in the Lord always.
I will say it again: Rejoice!

O Lord of my life, I am humbly grateful for all the days You have given me this past year. On my last birthday (anniversary, etc.) I secretly wondered if I would still be here to celebrate the passing of another year. You have been with me through all the trials I have encountered during past months, and I thank You for the wonderful gift of being alive at this special time. You truly have planned my future, and You give me strength to walk each day with You. I am in awe as I remember the times when all hope was gone and yet You lifted me out of the pit and protected me from all danger. You always provided for me as I continued my journey in the Valley. You are indeed a God of miracles.

I ask You now to bless us as a family as we celebrate once again. Please let our memories of desperate times make us all the more thankful, instead of overwhelming us with sorrow or morbid fear. May we rejoice in what You have done for us since our last celebration and in how You will continue to sustain us. I thank You, Lord, for Your mercies which provide for me an abundant life.

Cancer Milestones

As a family we rejoice in my cancer victories and remember them from year to year. For example, Merv usually buys a bouquet of flowers in early May to remind us of my initial cancer surgery (removal of kidney, adrenal gland, spleen) and together we thank God for allowing me to experience one more year of life. (In May of 1997, we celebrated eight years!)

There are other milestones in my ongoing battle with cancer. On March 16, 1997, we celebrated two years of life since I was told I had at most six months. It was wonderful to thank God for sustaining me in the midst of my health struggles. We feel it is important to turn these stressful times into happy, victorious memories.

Psalm 30:11-12
You turned my wailing into dancing; you removed my
sackcloth and clothed me with joy, that my heart may sing to you and
not be silent. O Lord my God, I will give you thanks forever.

1 Chronicles 16:12
Remember the wonders he has done, his miracles,
and the judgments he pronounced.

Psalm 77:11
I will remember the deeds of the Lord; yes,
I will remember your miracles of long ago.

Lord, You are my healer, and I marvel at how You have sustained me. You have provided excellent doctors who have helped me in my battle against cancer. Today I pause to remember that so many months (years) have passed since my surgery (tests, cobalt treatments, etc.) and I thank You for each new day You have given me.

You were with me back then, and You continue to walk with me as I face my very uncertain future. Your grace always was and always will be sufficient (2 Corinthians 12:9). I truly thank You that Your plan for my life has included this special day of remembering. My family and I celebrate in gratitude as we reach another milestone in our journey in the Valley.

Caring, Competent Doctors

Even though I have experienced misdiagnoses and doctor error, most of my physicians have been very competent and caring. My surgeons have been extremely skillful in their efforts to rid my body of cancer. While I consider God to be my Great Physician, I see these excellent doctors as a gift from Him. I have much confidence in them and know they have played a vital role in keeping my disease under control.

Over the years I have been under the care of a holistic physician, a chiropractor, a radiologist and two naturopathic doctors, in addition to my surgeons and oncologists. I continue to benefit from their combined expertise.

I especially appreciate those doctors who treat me as an informed individual with feelings rather than "just a number." My heart goes out to patients whose medical care has been less than adequate, realizing how blessed I am. I thank God regularly for the dedication and expertise of these very special men and women who care for and encourage me.

Philippians 1:3
I thank my God every time I remember you.

(Although I found no fitting scriptures about doctors, this one should remind us to pray for them often. I consider all biblical references to thanksgiving appropriate because I see my doctors as gifts from the Lord.)

Lord God, You are the Great Physician, source of my health and well-being. I thank You for the highly skilled doctors You have provided to help facilitate Your healing in my body. I have benefited much from their wisdom and care for me in my continuing battle with this wretched disease. I am grateful for the many years of study and sacrifice they have endured to become the competent health professionals they are today. I appreciate the time they have spent with me, not only offering treatments, but also encouraging me in my struggles. Forgive me when I take them for granted instead of thanking them for their care for me. Bless them all.

(Make a list of your doctors and pray for each by name.)

Everyday Blessings and Experiences

≈≈

When cancer strikes a family, everyone is profoundly affected. As appointments, hospital visits or stays, treatments, etc., rob us of time and energy, familiar family routines fall apart, frustration sets in and relationships are stressed. Add fear, discouragement, pain and uncertainty concerning the future, and the result can be a heavy atmosphere of negativism. It seems as if nothing is normal and probably never will be. The present is dark; the future looks darker.

I have found that prayers, especially those of gratitude, can dispel the gathering gloom. We may wonder what could possibly be left for which to be thankful when life seems to be crushing us on all sides.

One day, when I was in a particularly grumpy mood, I forced myself to make a list of all my blessings, and I learned a valuable lesson: there are always countless blessings (many of which I take for granted) no matter how grim the circumstances. I told Merv that I realized I would much rather be fighting cancer in North America than experiencing good health in countries like Bosnia or Rwanda. In spite of my illness, my life here is much more desirable than it would be in a war-torn, impoverished country. That day I thanked God for many things which I had never stopped to consider before.

Psalm 9:1
I will praise you, O Lord, with all my heart;
I will tell of all your wonders.

1 Thessalonians 5:18
Give thanks in all circumstances,
for this is God's will for you in Christ Jesus.

Psalm 107:1
Give thanks to the Lord, for he is good;
his love endures forever.

Psalm 13:5-6

But I trust in your unfailing love; my heart rejoices in your salvation. I will sing to the Lord, for he has been good to me.

O my Father, everything around me feels as if it is out of control and I am very frustrated. Nothing seems to be going as I had hoped. My cancer prognosis looks more dismal every day. Yet You tell me to give thanks at all times. Is this really possible? Open my eyes to see Your blessings in the ordinary things. Let me rejoice in them instead of dwelling on my losses which seem so great. Forgive me for grumbling and murmuring against You.

Accept my humble prayers of gratitude for:

...my spouse, children, home...

...forgiveness, salvation, the Bible...

...food, vitamins, supplements...

...hospitals, doctors, medical insurance...

...my senses of sight, touch, smell...

...ability to stand, walk, read, laugh, cry...

...Your promises of love, protection, wisdom...

(Let these ideas help you in your own prayer of thanksgiving for those things so often taken for granted.)

Financial Sufficiency

God has always provided for us, even though my battle with cancer has been very costly. Since substitute teaching has no health benefits, my paychecks stopped when, on the advice of my doctor, I quit my job. Our children attended university and college during our years in the Valley. Needless to say, their tuition and my therapies needed to be paid, but somehow the funds always were sufficient. I recall the day our son David needed to buy a car to go to Nova Scotia to continue his highly specialized, postgraduate education. Finances were tight, so when he saw my anxiety he said, "Don't worry, Mom. God never left us sitting at the curb yet!" I had never heard that expression before, but it encouraged me and reminded me to keep my eyes on the One who promises to provide.

When a CAT scan in June 1996 revealed many metastatic kidney cancer tumors in my liver and renal bed, as well as lymph node involvement in my pancreatic area, we knew I had a critical life-and-death battle ahead. As oncology had so little to offer, I again chose the complementary medical procedures. A very extreme detoxification and immune system boosting regime was initiated, and for several months the addition of "heavy-duty" enzymes, antioxidants and bowel cleansers pushed the cost to over six hundred dollars per month. It was possible to cope with the added expense because we had made our last mortgage payment the previous month. God's timing was perfect! My present monthly costs, including the expensive organic food I have been advised to eat, are still quite high but manageable.

It continues to frustrate us that our medical insurance pays for only a few of my supplements, etc., even though they all are prescribed by a medical doctor. Most are not accepted because they lack Drug Identification Numbers (DIN). This is the case with most herbal remedies. I continue to enjoy vibrant health in spite of my many metastases thanks to God's healing power and these costly items. This absolutely amazes those doctors who believe in neither.

We continue to thank God for providing the opportunity and financial resources to fight for my life in these ways.

God's promise to supply our needs certainly has been proven in our family many times as we've journeyed in the Valley. (Sometimes quite literally—in March 1997 our old Jetta diesel car "died" after traveling 463,000 kilometers! We believe God had a hand in its longevity.) We thank God daily for all His blessings and ask for His guidance in choosing the proper therapies. We trust He will provide whatever is needed.

Philippians 4:19
*And my God will meet all your needs according
to his glorious riches in Christ Jesus.*

Hebrews 13:5
*Keep your lives free from the love of money and be content
with what you have, because God has said,
"Never will I leave you; never will I forsake you."*

Psalm 55:22
*Cast your cares on the Lord and he will sustain you;
he will never let the righteous fall.*

Ecclesiastes 5:10a
*Whoever loves money never has money enough;
whoever loves wealth is never satisfied with his income.*

My Provider, I thank You for supplying all my needs in spite of the extra expense which fighting my disease has brought to our family. Thank you for teaching us to trust You for our financial needs instead of worrying about them. You indeed are a loving, caring Heavenly Father, and I ask Your forgiveness for all those times when I have fretted about our finances, choosing doubt instead of faith in Your ability to provide. Help me always to live at peace and in gratitude to You, remembering and rejoicing in how You have supplied everything we have needed at just the right time.

(List the times God has provided for your needs and enter into a time of thanksgiving.)

God's Promises

*T*hroughout my years in the Valley, I have received tremendous support and encouragement from my family and friends. Their loving words, acts of kindness and prayers have been invaluable. Even so, the most hope and encouragement comes from God Himself, through His Word and promises. I share just a few of my favorite ones. Take time to meditate on them and jot down how these promises have been evident in your own struggle with cancer. Ask the Lord to teach you how to live in victory in light of these words from Him. Thank Him for all the ways you personally have experienced these blessings and continue your journey in the joy of the Lord.

Salvation
John 3:16
For God so loved the world that he gave his one and only Son, that whoever believes in him shall not perish but have eternal life.

John 11:25-26
Jesus said to her, "I am the resurrection and the life. He who believes in me will live, even though he dies; and whoever lives and believes in me will never die. Do you believe this?"

Forgiveness
1 John 1:9
If we confess our sins, he is faithful and just and will forgive us our sins and purify us from all unrighteousness.

Mercy
Hebrews 4:16
Let us then approach the throne of grace with confidence, so that we may receive mercy and find grace to help us in our time of need.

Strength
Isaiah 40:29
*He gives strength to the weary and
increases the power of the weak.*

Wisdom
James 1:5
*If any of you lacks wisdom, he should ask God,
who gives generously to all without finding fault,
and it will be given to him.*

His presence
Matthew 28:20b
*"And surely I am with you always,
to the very end of the age."*

Peace
John 14:27
*"Peace I leave with you; my peace I give you.
I do not give to you as the world gives.
Do not let your hearts be troubled and do not be afraid."*

Direction
Proverbs 3:5-6
*Trust in the Lord with all your heart and lean not on
your own understanding; in all your ways
acknowledge him, and he will make your paths straight.*

Healing
Psalm 103:2-3
*Praise the Lord, O my soul, and forget not all his benefits—who
forgives all your sins and heals all your diseases.*

Isaiah 53:5b
…and by his wounds we are healed.

Good Health, Good Days

~ ~

*F*or some people, pain and much suffering are their daily experience from cancer diagnosis to death. However, most of us do have good days, even weeks and years, between cancer crises. I have had as long as two years of excellent health between some of my crises, but even during my periods of severe cancer struggles, there have been good days. Since my disease has been at the terminal stage for many years and CAT scans in June 1996 and June 1997 revealed many metastatic tumors in my liver and renal bed and several enlarged peripancreatic lymph nodes, every day is a miracle. My vibrant health and energy level continue to amaze my doctors.

I go to bed at night thankful for the privilege of having enjoyed another healthy, pain-free day. Each morning as I realize that I still feel healthy I again thank God for His wonderful grace and mercy in my life. Living one day at a time lets me see each day as a miraculous gift from my loving, caring Heavenly Father, and I strive to live it to the fullest in a spirit of gratitude. Everyone should live like that, but it seems to take a terminal illness to teach us how precious each day is.

Psalm 118:28-29
You are my God, and I will give you thanks;
you are my God, and I will exalt you. Give thanks to the
Lord, for he is good; his love endures forever.

2 Corinthians 12:9
But he said to me, "My grace is sufficient for you,
for my power is made perfect in weakness." Therefore I will
boast all the more gladly about my weaknesses,
so that Christ's power may rest on me.

Psalm 51:15
O Lord, open my lips, and my mouth will declare your praise.

*O*Heavenly Father, once again I am experiencing a wonderful, pain-free, crisis-free day. In light of my CAT scans and prognosis, this truly is a miracle from You. I stand in awe, and worship You for who You are and what You are doing for me. My life is in Your hands and I rejoice in Your continuing sustenance day by day.

Forgive me whenever I take my good health for granted, forgetting that You alone are the source of my well-being. Teach me to have a spirit of gratitude at all times, and show me how I should live each day to Your glory.

Help me reach out with Your love and comfort to those who are suffering today. When their Valley is dark and fearsome and their pain and doubts overwhelm them, let me be there for them. Equip me to be a holy channel of Your joy, comfort and peace.

Lord, I thank You that I know from previous crises that if my cancer flares up again, You will still be with me, just as You are right now. Even in sickness and pain You have always comforted me with Your love and compassion. Thank you for teaching me that truth many years ago when I first had cancer.

So now I will continue my journey today, rejoicing in You, my Savior. You are my All in All. When I have You, I truly have everything; my delight is in You.

Good Prognoses
(test results, etc.)

During my many years of battling cancer my prognoses have ranged from assurances that I had no living kidney cancer cells in my body because they had "got it all" to the opposite extreme in the form of a "six-month death sentence." Obviously, good reports need celebrations, and that is what we have usually done. I feel it is extremely important to make the most of a good report, for no one knows the time of the next crisis. Cancer is notorious for its recurring metastatic tumors.

When I am given good news we rejoice as a family and share our joy with friends who have been praying for me. We all thank God for His mercy. I also thank Him for being with me in the dark times too, knowing that if things should take a turn for the worse, He will still be with me. It only takes the discovery of one little lump to radically change a positive prognosis into another round of tests, biopsies, treatments or surgeries. I have made many rounds on that cancer "merry-go-round" over the years. Therefore, I consciously try to live a life of much gratitude to God when things are going well. Good prognoses are indeed a gift from Him. I tell my doctors that many people are praying for me and how important my faith is in dealing with this disease.

Psalm 86:13
For great is your love toward me; you have delivered
me from the depths of the grave.

Psalm 68:19-20
Praise be to the Lord, to God our Savior, who daily
bears our burdens. Our God is a God who saves;
from the Sovereign Lord comes escape from death.

Psalm 103:2
Praise the Lord, O my soul, and forget not all his benefits.

Psalm 51:15
O Lord, open my lips, and my mouth will declare your praise.

*M*y dearest Heavenly Father, I have no words to express my love and gratitude to You for the blessing of this good report. It has given me a new lease on life, and I rejoice with my family because we can once again plan for a future together. Thank you for answering all our prayers concerning the problems I have been facing.

Thank you, too, for being with me as I went through the tests (biopsies, etc.) and for giving me peace of mind. I am grateful You have taught me in Your Word that I need not worry when I give my burdens and cares to You. Bring that to my memory if a new crisis should happen. Thank you for being the same always: yesterday, today and forever (Hebrews 13:8).

Lord, teach me how to help, comfort and encourage others in the Valley whose prognoses seem hopeless. Let me bring Your hope to them in their despair. May I always give You all the glory, and may Your life shine through me. You are my All, and I trust You with my life. Thank you, Jesus.

Joy

God has blessed me with much joy, even on the dark days. I believe this comes from having an implicit childlike faith, which of course is a gift from Him. There seems to be a difference between simple happiness and the joy of the Lord. I do feel happy most of the time, but deep abiding joy is not necessarily dependent on the emotion we call happiness. To be happy in the face of a dismal prognosis or surgery is difficult if not impossible for me, but many times I have experienced His joy deep within, even in the most devastating circumstances. Usually it is His Word and my faith in it which rekindles the spark of joy in my spirit. Absolute trust brings peace and joy, for it reaches beyond this life.

Psalm 30:11
*You turned my wailing into dancing; you
removed my sackcloth and clothed me with joy.*

Psalm 28:6-7
*Praise be to the Lord, for he has heard my cry for mercy.
The Lord is my strength and my shield; my heart trusts in
him, and I am helped. My heart leaps for joy and
I will give thanks to him in song.*

Psalm 94:19
*When anxiety was great within me,
your consolation brought joy to my soul.*

O my God and Savior, I come to You with an indescribable feeling of joy welling up in my spirit as I realize that my future is Your concern, not mine. You know what is in store for me and I trust You, even in these days when my disease seems to be an insidious villain, determined to destroy my body, the temple of Your Holy Spirit.

I thank You for these gifts of joy and faith which strengthen me as I spend another day in the Valley. In its depths I can only look up, and looking up I see light, beauty, and sometimes even a rainbow. These direct my thoughts toward You, for You are the Light of the world shining through all darkness. The "rainbow experiences" bring to mind Your promises. How blessed I am to know You as the giver of joy and sustainer of my life.

Enable me to share Your joy with others, especially those for whom the Valley is very dark. Show them Your light, hope and joy. I rejoice and worship You, not only for what You do for me, but more so, for who You are—my Lord, Healer, Savior and my Joy. Without You I would be in the deep pit of despair. How can I thank You?

Laughter, A Good Sense of Humor

I have always considered a good sense of humor as a gift from the Lord. Life without laughter would be unimaginably dull and somber, so even while living with terminal cancer I choose to see humor in many aspects of my life.

For example, my coffee retention enemas have been known as "Mom's coffee break" ever since another cancer warrior told me her husband said it gives a whole new meaning to coffee breaks. Our family and close friends have thought up our own jokes about that liver-detoxing procedure, and I have come to accept "coffee breaks" as part of my routine. My friends laugh when I tell them I'll call my next book Coffee Stains in My Toilet Bowl!

My keen sense of humor allows my friends to be themselves, and we are free to share new jokes with one another. My laughter puts them at ease and reduces the tension they might feel because of my illness.

Laughter is thought to increase the flow of endorphins. These substances are very conducive to good health and general well-being. In fact, they are said to relieve pain because of the similarity in their chemical structure to morphine. What a pleasant pill to swallow!

Life is too short to go around with a long face, wallowing in self-pity. Furthermore, it is downright unhealthy and totally unenjoyable. (I must add that for those whose suffering is extreme, laughter may not be an option. I do not joke with them unless they initiate the frivolity or they may see it as a lack of compassion. I treat each person as an individual, respecting different personalities.)

Proverbs 17:22
A cheerful heart is good medicine,
but a crushed spirit dries up the bones.

Ecclesiastes 3:4
...a time to weep and a time to laugh.

Psalm 126:2
Our mouths were filled with laughter,
our tongues with songs of joy.

Proverbs 15:13
A happy heart makes the face cheerful,
but heartache crushes the spirit.

O Lord, You are the giver of all good gifts, and I thank You for my sense of humor which lightens up my days in the Valley. It allows me to have so many jolly times with my family and friends. I feel blessed because they know me well enough to include me in their fun in spite of my health problems. That helps me feel normal, for if everyone looked sad and spoke only of my illness I would sink into the sea of despair and gloom. Thank you, too, for their sensitivity in those times when I just can't laugh because the crisis I am facing is too great.

I ask You to continue blessing me with times of laughter and joy. May my happiness make other cancer patients' time in the Valley more enjoyable, too. Always help me to discern when to lighten our discussions with a bit of humor. For some, the days of laughter are long gone, for no one dares to joke in their presence. Show their friends that sick people need to experience the healing touch of laughter, too.

And so I thank You once again for refreshing me with Your gift of a good sense of humor and for giving me friends who make me laugh.

Peace

Peace, like joy, faith and hope, is a wonderful supernatural gift from our Heavenly Father. His peace is available to us even in the Valley, where it flows abundantly in spite of our circumstances. Some of my most profound feelings of peace have occurred during the most devastating times. God really does supply His peace if we truly desire it.

In June of 1997, just after receiving the news that a CAT scan revealed new liver tumors, I prayed for wisdom and asked God to encourage me with an appropriate word from my promise box. The card I chose had the following two scriptures: *Your ears shall hear a word behind you saying, "This is the way, walk in it," whenever you turn to the right hand or whenever you turn to the left* (Isaiah 30:21 NKJV). *So you shall serve the Lord your God, and He will bless your bread and your water. And I will take sickness from the midst of you* (Exodus 23:25 NKJV). Those scriptures gave me much peace, even though I did not know how God would work them out in my life.

One of my strategies for keeping my mind at peace before medical appointments is to sing praise songs in my car on the way to the doctor. When there, I pray instead of reading the outdated magazines. This focuses my thoughts on the Lord and His peace that passes all understanding.

I rejoice when I experience the peace of God, and endeavor to pass it on to others whose fear of cancer has blocked it out.

Isaiah 26:3
You will keep in perfect peace him whose mind is steadfast, because he trusts in you.

Proverbs 14:30
A heart at peace gives life to the body, but envy rots the bones.

John 14:27
Peace I leave with you; my peace I give you.
I do not give to you as the world gives.
Do not let your hearts be troubled and do not be afraid.

Colossians 3:15
Let the peace of Christ rule in your hearts, since as members
of one body you were called to peace. And be thankful.

O Lord of my life, thank you for Your wonderful, comforting gift of peace. Around me the lab reports and doctors' prognoses are screaming pain, discouragement and hopelessness, and yet I have peace, Your peace. "How is this possible?" I ask, knowing the answer lies in You, the God of miracles. Thank you for this peace that transcends all understanding (Philippians 4:7).

I do thank You for walking with me in the Valley, making it a peaceful journey today. Help those whose lives I touch, to feel and experience Your peace as it flows through me. Be glorified in my life as I face my very uncertain future with confidence in You.

Increase my desire to live a life of thankfulness in the face of all my troubles. With You as my guide, healer and Savior, I have so much for which to be thankful.

(Make a list including family, friends, competent doctors, medication, food, clothing, church, etc., for which you can thank God and spend time in prayers of gratitude to your loving Heavenly Father.)

Seasonal Changes

*T*ime takes on new meaning for the person fighting serious illness. In my struggle with terminal cancer, I'd often like to speed up time to quickly get through an imminent crisis. At times of stress the days seem to drag. At other times I would like to slow down the days because everything is going too fast.

One source of great joy is seeing one season give way to another. This reminds me that I have survived another period of time. In March 1995, when my oncologist gave me a "six-month death sentence," the ground was still covered with much snow, and I wondered if I would be well enough to walk in the beautiful spring weather.

Well, spring came and I reveled in its beauty. My walks were praise times as I thanked God for His mercy in allowing me to enjoy that season. The day I replaced my winter boots with sneakers was unforgettable!

Then summer arrived and I was grateful for another glorious season. But would I still be walking when the autumn leaves transformed my daily route into an exotic wonderland of colour? Would I hear the rustle of fallen leaves under my feet? My good health continued as I fought my battle, and I did have the joy of walking in those leaves.

That fall the first snowfall came very early at the end of October. While everyone else complained bitterly, I was secretly filled with delight. I had survived spring, summer and fall, and now it looked like winter. Putting my boots on again was very special. Even though I knew it was less than eight months, I felt as though a whole year had passed since that fateful day in March. I eagerly anticipated walking through another season. I continue to thank God for each new season He allows me to experience.

Ecclesiastes 3:1
There is a time for everything, and a season for
every activity under heaven.

Psalm 31:14-15a
But I trust in you, O Lord; I say, "You are my God."
My times are in your hands.

Psalm 57:11
Be exalted, O God, above the heavens;
let your glory be over all the earth.

O Lord, You have created such a magnificent world. My illness has given me a deeper appreciation for the beauty of the ever-changing seasons. You continue to give me the health I need to fully enjoy them.

My walks in winter are cold and invigorating, and I thank You for supplying the strength and energy I need to meet the challenge of cold, blustery weather.

When spring comes I marvel as the snow melts and plants peek through the ground once more and tiny leaves form a canopy overhead. The birds, which have returned, sing songs of joy as I walk in the refreshing beauty of spring.

You have blessed me with the heat and fun of summer. I thank You for keeping me in good health during our visits with family and friends. There are so many activities to enjoy and I am grateful for all of them. Even pulling weeds in our garden gives me much joy. Forgive me when in good health I have taken my ability to participate in these activities for granted.

As summer days cool and autumn colours change the landscape, I again sing songs of praise to You. The crisp air and screaming bluejays fill my heart with joy and the anticipation of another season.

When soft, white flakes gently cover the earth, winter arrives again. All this points to the fact that You have gifted me with another year of life with my loved ones and I will celebrate another Christmas with them. How can I ever thank You adequately for Your blessings?